KATHARINA ZECHLIN

creative
ENAMELLING
and jewelry-making

STERLING PUBLISHING CO., INC. NEW YORK

Oak Tree Press Co., Ltd. Distributed by WARD LOCK, Ltd., London & Sydney

OTHER BOOKS OF INTEREST

Abstract Art

Creating from Scrap

Creative Claywork

Express Yourself in Drawing

Cardboard Crafting

Ceramics—and How to Decorate Them

Designs—and How to Use Them

How to Make Things Out of Paper

Make Your Own Mobiles

Making Mosaics

Painting Portraits

Papier Mâché—and How to Use It

Printing as a Hobby

Tin-Can Crafting

PICTURE CREDITS

The author and publisher wish to thank the Metropolitan Museum of Art, New York, for the following photographs: on page 4, Plaque, The Crucifixion, The Michael Friedsam Collection, 1931; page 6, Figure of a cock, Gift of Edward G. Kennedy, 1929; page 6, Wine pot, Gift of Edward G. Kennedy, 1929; page 48, Figure, one of a pair, Gift of A. W. Bahr, 1954; page 52, Plaque, St. Simeon holding the Christ Child, Gift of Anne Payne Blumenthal, 1938. Thanks are also due to the Allcraft Tool and Supply Company, New York, for the photographs on pages 10, 12, 13, 14, 17, 18, 19 and 25.

Special thanks are due to Miss Florence Nach for her invaluable advice and assistance.

Translated by Paul Kuttner

Revised and adapted by Jennifer Mellen

Fifth Printing, 1970

Copyright © 1965 by

Sterling Publishing Co., Inc.

419 Park Avenue South, New York, N.Y. 10016

British edition published by Oak Tree Press Co., Ltd.

Distributed in Great Britain and the Commonwealth by

Ward Lock, Ltd., 116 Baker Street, London W1

Translated from the German, © 1965, Sixth Edition by Verlag Frech, Stuttgart

Manufactured in the United States of America   *All rights reserved*

Library of Congress Catalog Card No.: 65-20877

ISBN 0-8069-5062-5   UK 7061 2018 3

5063-3

Contents

WHAT IS ENAMEL?.. 5

MAKING A SIMPLE PENDANT.. 7
"Cleaning" the Metal . . . Applying the Powdered Enamel . . . Firing the Enamel . . . "Cooling" the Enamel

WHAT YOU WILL NEED.. 12
Pre-Formed Parts . . . Kilns . . . Glass-Domed Kilns . . . Bunsen and Butane Gas Burners . . . Larger Kilns . . . Adhesive . . . Other Equipment

ENAMELS 21
How to Purchase Enamels . . . Storing Enamel Powders . . . Making Color Samples

STENCILLED COASTERS 27
Applying a Base Coat . . . Making a Stencil . . . Applying a Stencil Design

FILING 31

A GAY COUNTER-ENAMELLED BOWL 32
Simultaneous Counter-Enamelling . . . Counter-Enamelling One Side at a Time

A "SURPRISE" TEXTURED ASH TRAY... 37

A FLOWERED PEN-AND-PENCIL TRAY... 43

A LUMINOUS LEAF BROOCH... 45

COLOR PLATES.. 49–56

A PICTURESQUE VEINED NUT DISH... 57

"PROFESSIONAL" ABSTRACT CUFF LINKS... 60
How to Clean Metal with Acid . . . Enamelling on an Acid-Cleaned Surface . . . How to Store Your Acid Cleaning Solution

A "SCRATCHED" LINK BRACELET... 65

A PAIR OF GEOMETRIC EARRINGS... 67
How to Solder

A GOLDEN CRACKLE PLATE... 70

WASHING ENAMEL POWDERS.. 74

A SILVER LEAF DISH.. 75

A GLEAMING PENDANT MADE WITH "LEFT-OVERS".. 79

A JEWELLED BROOCH.. 83

A SIMPLE CLOISONNÉ ASH TRAY... 87
Making a Cloisonné Design . . . Applying a Cloisonné Design . . . Wet Application of Enamel

THE CHAMPLEVÉ TECHNIQUE IN PICTURES... 98

COMMON FLAWS AFTER FIRING AND HOW TO CORRECT THEM.................. 101

INDEX 103

This 16th century French enamel plaque, entitled "The Crucifixion," is one of the finest examples of the Limoges school. Its colors are as brilliant today as they were when the plaque was made.

What Is Enamel?

Enamelling is the technique by which colored glass is melted and fused on to a metal base. The combination of fused glass and metal is called enamel. The glass used for enamelling is a special kind, for ordinary glass would crack as it cooled and spoil the beauty of the finished enamel creation. Since this special glass is colorless, metallic oxides are added to it to give it color: for example, cobalt oxide dyes the glass blue, copper oxide turns it green, and iron oxide turns it red or brown. Colors and shades of enamel run into the thousands, but, happily for you, you do not have to grind and mix the colors yourself. Choosing from a vast palette of colors, you can buy your enamels all prepared and ready to use in powder form—unlike the enamellists of ancient times who had to be chemists, as well as artists.

Enamelling is a very ancient craft, and the work of Chinese and Egyptian artists has endured throughout the centuries. You can still see the wonderful objects they wrought in museums throughout the world. In ancient Egypt, enamelling was used for jewelry, and Chinese vases thousands of years old still retain their sparkle and beauty. The Byzantines brought enamelling to a high degree of perfection from the fifth to the tenth centuries, with colors of unsurpassed richness. If you ever go to Venice, be sure to see one of their masterpieces, the "Pala d'Oro" in St. Mark's Cathedral, composed of 81 enamelled plaques. It always brings gasps of pleasure and wonderment from its beholders.

Enamelling flourished in Germany in the twelfth century in monasteries along the Rhine. French works from Limoges are popular with visitors to the Louvre and Cluny Museums in Paris.

A beautiful example of Benvenuto Cellini's art, an intricate chalice, is on

(Left) This cloisonné cock is an 18th century work of art of the Ch'ien Lung period. It is especially interesting because the cloisonné "cells" are elongated and rectangular, rather than traditionally tiny and round. (Right) Cloisonné enamel on copper gilt, this Chinese wine pot is of the Ming Dynasty (1368–1643).

display at the Metropolitan Museum of Art in New York. There is a legend about this famous eccentric enamellist, which is no doubt true. In order to keep his furnace going when he ran out of fuel at a crucial moment, he burnt up the furniture, despite his poor wife's pleas.

But with gas and electricity at your disposal, you will never have to burn up your furniture for fuel! Inexpensive kilns and pre-formed metal shapes to enamel on are readily available, thanks to modern technology, so you can create wonderful and enduring enamelled objects with a minimum of work and equipment. By working and experimenting in enamelling a little, you will soon become familiar with its possibilities. As to the techniques, that is what this book is for. Here are detailed step-by-step instructions, plus a materials checklist for each project. We suggest that you study each one carefully before you begin.

To show you just how easy enamelling is, without further ado we will explain how to make a simple pendant, postponing for the following chapter a more detailed discussion of materials and equipment.

Making a Simple Pendant

Materials Checklist

pre-formed copper disc with hole near one edge
small bottle opaque enamel powder, color optional
80-mesh strainer, or strainer-top to fit enamel bottle
clean white paper
kiln, butane gas burner, or Bunsen burner

Cleaning Materials:
1 cup vinegar
$1\frac{1}{2}$ tablespoons salt
pair of tweezers
fine emery paper or steel wool
clean cloth

Firing Materials:
asbestos gloves
asbestos board or brick
   or refractory stone
small shovel-shaped spatula
   or
enamelling fork with shield

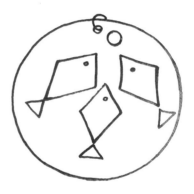

Always assemble the things you will need before you start to enamel, since it could be very frustrating to have to look for some urgently needed material while the enamel is in the kiln and needs attention. If you do not have a work table, protect the table you will be working on with one or two layers of newspaper, and spread clean white paper over this. Place your kiln or burner in one corner of the table, and keep your spatula or enamelling fork and asbestos gloves handy next to it at all times to transport pieces to and from the kiln. Be sure the kiln rests securely on the sturdiest corner of

7

your work table to prevent its toppling over, and you may want to protect the table top by placing an asbestos mat under the kiln. Have your small bottles of powdered enamel ready nearby in one or two neat rows.

"CLEANING" THE METAL

Cleanliness is one of the essential factors for successful enamelling, as your own experience will soon teach you. Enamel will not adhere to any metal surface that is not perfectly clean, so your first step will always be to clean *meticulously* the metal surface to be enamelled. Later on, we will discuss various methods of cleaning, but for now the following simple "pickling" solution is sufficient: Drop the copper pendant into a glass bowl containing 1 cup of vinegar to which you have added 1½ tablespoonsful of ordinary table salt, and leave it there until it is clean and shiny. This should take one or two minutes. Then polish the surface with fine emery paper, and wipe it with a perfectly clean cloth. Do not touch the metal surface with your fingers at any time, but instead use a pair of tweezers which you have "cleaned" in the vinegar solution. Holding the pendant carefully with these, by its very edges, place it on a piece of immaculate white paper, rough side up. (The rough side of copper will usually have a barely visible black ring near the edge of the disc.) This side is placed uppermost for enamelling because the rough, slightly raised edge holds the enamel powder better near the edge.

APPLYING THE POWDERED ENAMEL

For this first project, use a single layer of enamel in a single opaque color. If the color you have selected comes in a bottle with a sprinkler-lid, simply remove the outer lid. If not, shake a small amount of powder into the 80-mesh strainer. Now sprinkle the powdered enamel over the prepared or "clean" metal surface as regularly as possible. The best way to obtain an even coating is to tap the slightly inclined bottle or strainer with your index finger, instead of shaking your whole hand. Sprinkle the edges of the pendant a little more heavily.

Continue sprinkling slowly until you have a layer of enamel which is roughly as thick as the metal itself. A layer thicker than the metal will often

The best way to obtain an even coating is to tap the slightly inclined shaker with your index finger. Before firing the pendant, remove all enamel powder from the hole which will receive the jump ring, or the enamel will seal it during the firing process.

result in a broken piece, while a too-thin layer will result in cracks, fissures and unsightly bubbles. So always take special care to enamel evenly (except for the edges) until you reach the proper thickness. Each color has special characteristics, which you will discover as you use them, but in general, red colors require a thicker layer of enamel than others.

FIRING THE ENAMEL

If you are going to use a kiln, it must be pre-heated to 1500° F., so turn it on ahead of time. A gas burner does not need to be pre-heated.

When your pendant has an even layer of enamel except for the built-up edges, carefully slide your spatula or enamelling fork under it, or place the pendant on the spatula with the aid of a pair of clean tweezers. Remember not to touch any part of the enamelled surface with your fingers at any time, and to *wear asbestos gloves whenever you use the kiln.*

Place the enamelled pendant in the pre-heated kiln, and carefully withdraw the spatula or enamelling fork. (Remember to use asbestos gloves.)

The moment of greatest excitement in enamelling comes as you peer

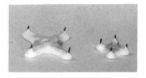

Firing stilts such as these are used to support objects such as jewelry, coasters, bowls and plates while they are in the kiln. Almost all enamelled objects must be supported on a stilt of some kind during the firing process to prevent damage to the enamel surface and to the kiln.

through the window or glass cover of your kiln to watch the dull, powdery surface of your pendant turn into gleaming, glistening enamel. At first you will see the surface become granular, and the powder itself will change colors. Little by little the entire surface liquefies. When it becomes smooth and brilliant, and the metal itself is heated to a light red (in a kiln, this will take anywhere from 2 to 4 minutes, with a Bunsen or butane gas burner, slightly longer), the firing process is complete. Then (wearing gloves) remove it with your spatula, and place it on a piece of asbestos (or refractory stone) to finish cooling completely.

"COOLING" THE ENAMEL

The temperature in your room must be kept constant during cooling because a sudden air current or change in temperature can lead to irreparable cracks or fissures in the enamel. Guard, too, against inadvertently sprinkling water on the hot enamel.

As the enamel cools, you will see a constant change of colors. Watching this color mutation is one of the more exciting facets of enamelling. Only after the pendant has cooled enough to touch with bare hands will it show the color it will always retain.

How did your firing succeed? If the surface shows signs of dents or air bubbles and dark holes, you can assume that the sprinkling of enamel was too light. In this case, you can correct the glaze simply by sprinkling again and firing your pendant a second time. All enamelled objects are fired several times, and even a single-color object usually requires 2 or 3 sprinklings and firings, so do not worry if you have to re-sprinkle and re-fire. The second and third firings, performed the same way, should last only about one to two minutes at the same temperature.

Blackened, burned rims tell you that the first firing attempt lasted too long. On the other hand, if the surface is rough and uneven you fired the pendant too short a time. Over-firing cannot be corrected, but if the pendant is under-fired you can fire it again.

Let us hope that your pendant cools to a lovely, even color. Now all it needs is a jump ring and a chain, and it is ready to wear.

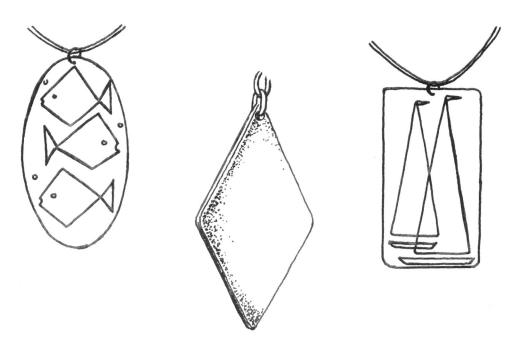

After the pendant is fired and cool, add a jump ring and a chain and it is ready to wear.

11

What You Will Need

PRE-FORMED PARTS

Pre-formed copper shapes are readily available from any enamelling supplier, and need only be thoroughly cleaned before you enamel on them. Ash trays, cuff links, bracelets, trays, plates, earrings, necklaces, rings, cups and plaques are only a few of the inexpensive shapes available in a wide variety of sizes. With a few pre-formed copper parts you will be able to complete any of the projects in this book. Although many professionals shape their own metal parts, this is a craft in itself, and you should concentrate on learning the techniques of enamelling before attempting it.

You will also need a small selection of what are called "findings" (cuff link and earring backs, chains and jump rings for pendants, brooch backs and so on).

Copper is the metal most frequently employed in enamelling. It is relatively inexpensive, and is available in the widest variety of sizes and shapes.

Delicate link bracelets, fishes, leaves and tiny animals are more examples of the pre-formed shapes available to the enamellist today.

These pre-formed, ready-to-enamel copper shapes represent only a small selection of the many inexpensive parts available in all sizes and shapes.

Another major advantage is copper's ability to withstand as many as ten successive firings without losing its shape.

Fine silver and sterling silver can be enamelled successfully, but since these metals are so costly it is best to work with copper until you are proficient in the techniques of enamelling. Silver is available in similar shapes to copper. Gold, platinum and steel are also suitable for enamelling, but are difficult to work with and extremely expensive.

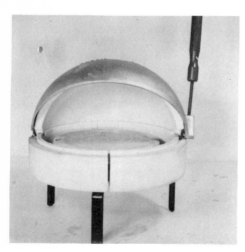

Small round kilns are available in many different styles, such as those pictured here. Highly recommended for beginners, they are large enough to accommodate jewelry, small dishes, coasters and ash trays. They are inexpensive, simple to work with, and give excellent results.

KILNS

Since enamelling is an "art of fire," the kiln or oven is the most important piece of equipment to the enamellist. The softest enamel enters into fusion at not less than 1380° F., and kilns can reach a temperature of 2000° F.

Several kinds of kilns are available. They range from quite inexpensive small kilns resembling hot plates to elaborate and very expensive ceramic furnaces and kilns. Large expensive kilns are not necessary or even desirable for a beginner, however, and even the most modestly priced kiln is completely satisfactory for firing enamel. Most of your enamel creations will be quite small, so a large kiln would be superfluous; in addition, large kilns waste electricity, require an overlong warm-up period, and most of all prevent you from viewing the firing process, the most exciting facet of enamelling.

Glass-Domed Kilns

A simple and inexpensive kiln consists of a small round electric coil heater, which comes equipped with a heat-resistant glass bell to go over it, as well as a lid made of metal. The glass lid retains the heat so well that the temperature within the little kiln becomes intense. By topping the glass lid with the metal bell cover, you can increase the heat still further, but this heat increase does not outweigh the disadvantage of obscuring the firing process.

You need a tool to serve as a handle for manipulating the lid. It can work on a leverage principle, or by clamping, as with a pair of tongs. With this kiln, you can even interrupt the firing, if necessary, to make a change in your enamelling designs.

The working surface of such a kiln is usually about 5 or 6 inches in diameter, and has a device which prevents the enamelled pieces from coming in direct contact with the heating element. Some models have a grille, and others cover the heating element entirely with a metal plate.

The electricity which heats the kiln does so by passing through wire coils known as resistances, because they offer resistance to the current flowing through them. This, in turn, causes friction, and friction—as you well know if you have ever had a rope-burn—causes heat, especially if it is continuous. Friction also tends to wear things out, however, so it is not a good idea to use your kiln for long periods of time without interruption. Even without excessive use, the heating element has only a limited life expectancy, and if you use the kiln often, you will probably have to change the element about every 6 months.

Bunsen and Butane Gas Burners

Firing with a Bunsen gas burner is a method which is often used commercially, as well as by the experienced studio enamellist. Its great drawback is that the open gas flames are potentially dangerous, and the method is definitely unsuitable for use with children. Another disadvantage is that this method of firing is really suitable only for jewelry, as even objects as small as an ash tray tend to receive an uneven application of heat, and look lumpy and awkward when completed.

In a studio equipped with gas and supplied with burners and a ring stand, this method is simple and practical. It, too, allows you to watch the firing process, and to interrupt it at any time when necessary. This is how it works:

Clamp a ring about 4 inches in diameter to the ring stand. Place a Bunsen burner beneath the ring (the Bunsen burner may be replaced by a handheld butane gas burner/torch) so that its flame will be directed towards the object to be enamelled. To prevent the open flame from touching the enamelled object (though as we will explain later on this is sometimes done to achieve special decorative effects), you must place an asbestos plate on the ring, or use a firing stand covered with steel netting. Objects to be fired are placed on top of the asbestos plate. As there is no way to determine exact temperatures with an open flame, objects must be fired until they fuse. This is another disadvantage of this method which beginners would do well to avoid.

An inexpensive butane gas burner has several distinct advantages over the Bunsen burner for the beginner. Since it comes with its own supply of gas in a little tank, an expensive gas connection is not necessary. Small in

(Left) This is how Bunsen burners are set up for firing. The object to be fired is placed on a metal plate, and heat is applied from below. (Right) An inexpensive stand and wire mesh square can be used to support pieces while firing with a Bunsen burner. The holes in the mesh allow sufficient heat to reach the enamel.

size, the butane gas burner is light in weight and also comes equipped with its own stand. It can be used anywhere—in the kitchen, in the bedroom, in the playroom, and even out-of-doors. It is used just like the Bunsen burner.

Larger Kilns

If you want to enamel objects which are larger than jewelry, trays or small dishes, for example, you will not be able to fire them in the small kilns we have described so far. Or, if you want to produce small objects in large quantities, you will want a kiln which holds many pieces at a time.

Commercial box-type kilns are designed to produce high temperatures with the least possible expenditure of electricity. They are insulated with fire-brick, which makes them quite heavy and bulky, although a kiln with inside dimensions no larger than 8 x 8 x 5 inches would still be portable. These kilns plug into an ordinary electric socket, and all come with detailed firing instructions.

17

Commercial, box-type kilns range from simple to relatively elaborate ones. This kiln is equipped with a pyrometer (right), which indicates the interior temperature and also turns the kiln off automatically.

These kilns are far more expensive than the small round kilns with domed lids. Some come equipped with a pyrometer which can shut them off automatically, a useful but fairly expensive device.

ADHESIVE

Objects with steep walls such as bowls, bracelets, ash trays and vases must be "painted" with an adhesive so that the enamel will stick to the sides and not run down during the firing process. The most common adhesive is gum tragacanth. This adhesive is readily available, and comes in yellow or grey lumps, flakes, or ribbon-like pieces. It must be soaked overnight in water and then (after you add enough water so that it will not burn) you cook it until it becomes more fluid. After it has cooled, more water can be added and the entire mixture strained through a 200-mesh sieve or cheesecloth. The gum should be as thin and clear as water when applied to enamel and metal surfaces, and it is important to apply it thinly and evenly.

Gum tragacanth, as well as other adhesives such as a new "super" gum, is also available in ready-to-use form. These prepared adhesives are, of course, more costly, but you may find that their convenience makes up for their additional cost, especially since adhesives play a major rôle in the art of enamelling.

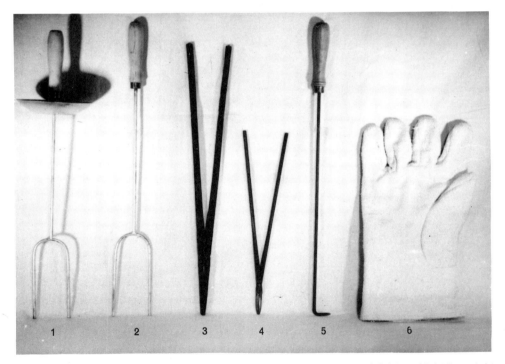

Enamelling forks (1, 2) and tongs (3, 4) are essential aides to successful firing. Light in weight and inexpensive, they also ensure complete safety. A scrolling iron (5) is an inexpensive "extra" for special effects. Asbestos gloves (6) are indispensable for handling hot objects as they come from the kiln.

(Left) This group of enamelled objects illustrates the vast range of decorative techniques available to achieve interesting effects. Bits of glass, iridescent enamels, and stencils were used.

Two of the three counter-enamelled objects on the right were further embellished with stencil applications. The counter-enamelled Arabic hammered ash tray on the left is an antique.

OTHER EQUIPMENT

None! You really do not need anything else at all. With a small selection of enamel powders and perhaps a tiny assortment of lumps and threads, a little kiln or burner, adhesive, and a few pre-formed metal parts, you will be able to complete—successfully—every project in this book, and more. Ordinary household objects such as toothpicks, vinegar, and even pocket combs will come in handy as "tools" for special effects, but expensive tools and heavy equipment are not necessary or even recommended. Your only additional "tools" will be enthusiasm, care, and a desire to learn more about one of the most fascinating crafts in the world, enamelling.

Enamels

There are three different kinds of enamel:

The opaque (covering enamels)

The transparent (translucent enamels)

The opalescent (clouded or milky enamels)

Opaque enamels completely cover the metal on which they are fired, and do not allow the metal color underneath to show through. Therefore, opaque enamels are especially suited for inexpensive metals such as copper and pinchbeck (an alloy of copper and 10–15 % zinc), and for under-coatings when several enamel layers are desired.

Transparent enamels, as the name implies, permit the color underneath to show through. They are used over opaque enamels, directly on clean copper, and to enamel such precious metals as silver and gold, achieving an effect resembling stained glass.

Opalescent enamels give the appearance of transparency, and have a strangely shimmering effect. They are not as "glassy" and clear as the transparent enamels, nor as simple and opaque as the covering enamels. Depending on the way light hits them, they reflect an unusual and mysterious glow. These seldom-used enamels come in only a few colors when they are available at all, but since opaque and transparent enamels come in such a large variety of sparkling colors you will not feel at all limited by the lack of opalescents.

HOW TO PURCHASE ENAMELS

Enamel is melted in factories in huge jars, poured out and, when cool, cracked into enormous blocks. Ground to a fine powder, it is then sold to the trade in various forms. The best (and easiest) way to buy enamel is in ready-to-use powder form, ground to 80-mesh (that is, the enamel powder will pass through a sieve which contains 80 square openings to the inch). Enamels in lump form and in unwashed powder form are less expensive than fully prepared powders, but these involve a great deal of tedious work and, in the washing process, lose up to 50 % in volume, so you do not really save anything in the end.

At first you will need a selection of 80-mesh powdered enamels. Little balls, tiny lumps and threads of enamel are also useful for decorative effects. As you develop more skill and begin to use more advanced techniques, you will need enamel ground as fine as face powder (200-mesh) for enamel brush-work painting, and enamels which are somewhat different in composition from copper enamels for enamelling on silver and other precious metals.

STORING ENAMEL POWDERS

You will probably find that the enamel colors you buy come in neat little jars with labels on them. If, however, you get paper bags or envelopes of powders, you will need a clean empty bottle or small jar with a tight cap for each color. You must keep your enamel powders tightly capped at all times to prevent impurities from invading the colors and spoiling an enamelled object. Each jar must be carefully labelled with the name of the color, kind of enamel (opaque, transparent or opalescent), firing characteristics (we will explain this later on), and the manufacturer's number. Your labels should look like this:

Opaque Light Blue
#314—B
Medium-fusing

There are 3 vital reasons for labelling your jars in this way:

1. Manufacturers often change the descriptive names of the various enamels as new shades and hues are developed, but invariably retain each color's original number. Thus, if a manufacturer has been advertising Opaque Light Blue #314–B, and he develops additional blue shades, he may change the title "Opaque Light Blue" to "Opaque Pale Blue" but will retain #314–B since the color is identical to the original. If you use the

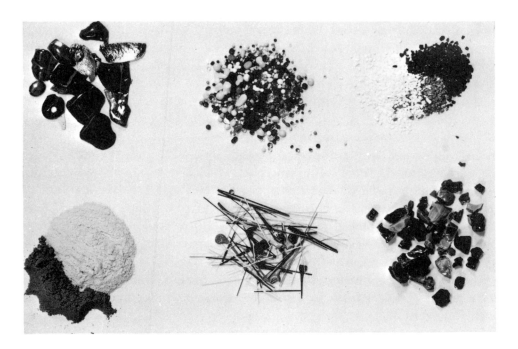

Enamel is available in several forms. Lumps and threads, which come in various sizes, are very effective as decorative accents. Below, left, is enamel powder ground to 200-mesh (it will pass through a sieve with 200 openings to the inch), which is used for enamel brush-work-painting decoration.

manufacturer's number when re-ordering, you will always receive the right tint or color gradation, regardless of the name.

2. One of enamelling's cardinal rules is that *you cannot mix either colors or kinds of enamels* the way that oil or water-color paints are mixed. You cannot add blue to yellow and obtain green, for instance, or add a touch of dark red to a light red, for the two colors would still remain distinct from each other after firing. Neither can you mix transparent and opaque enamels to obtain opalescent enamels, or to achieve an effective combination. Enamels are available in a profusion of colors, and almost every imaginable gradation of color, so you will never find this a disadvantage.

23

3. Not all enamels react in the same way to the firing process, and it is important to experiment with the enamels you purchase, investigating their habits under different circumstances before starting any project. Even enamel colors within the same family will have vastly different peculiarities, so it is a good idea to find out just what you can and cannot do with each shade and hue. There are three enamel fusing categories:

Soft-fusing (sometimes called low-firing) enamels "mature" (become smooth and glossy) when they are fired at a relatively low (1400° F.) temperature for 2 to 4 minutes. These soft enamels are used over hard enamels to produce various decorative effects. A soft enamel must be applied thicker than a hard enamel, since soft enamels burn away quickly. If several layers of enamel are to be applied to an object, soft enamels are applied last, or they would burn away by the time the object was fired 4 or 5 times. Tiny enamel decorative lumps and threads are usually soft-firing.

Medium-fusing (or medium-firing) enamels mature when they are fired at 1450° to 1500° F. for 2 to 4 minutes, and are the enamels you will use most frequently.

Hard-fusing (or hard-firing) enamels mature when they are fired at 1600° F. for 2 to 4 minutes, and are the most durable of all enamels. Hard enamels are used when an object is to be fired many times, and are preferred for "counter-enamelling" (the protective enamel coating on the back or underside of an object).

Although many manufacturers have developed soft-, medium-, and hard-firing enamels in certain colors (notably black, white and clear transparent enamels), many colors are either soft, medium or hard because of their chemical make-up. For example, all opaque reds and oranges and many blacks and whites tend to be soft, low-firing enamels, while opaque beiges are usually hard-firing. Opaque ivories, lavenders and yellows are slightly less hard-firing than beiges, and transparent enamels tend to be hard-firing, though they are affected by the color underneath them. All transparent colors benefit from several firings, that is, they become clearer, lighter and more luminous each time they are fired. If transparent enamels are used for counter-enamelling, be sure to test them for hardness, as soft enamels are not suitable for counter-enamelling.

24

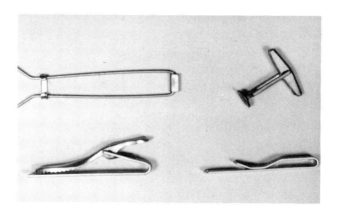

"Findings" for jewelry come in many styles, such as this selection of brooch and cuff link backs.

MAKING COLOR SAMPLES

To avoid costly mistakes and guesswork the simplest thing to do is fire a small test sample of every color as you buy it, and glue the little sample to its corresponding bottle of enamel. Simply sprinkle the powdered enamel over a perfectly clean square of copper and fire it. Watch the sample while it is being fired, and as soon as it turns smooth and glossy it is done. If the enamel melts and fuses at 1400° F. it is a soft enamel, at 1450° or 1500° F. it is a medium enamel, and at 1600° F. it is a hard enamel. Add this information to the label on the bottle, and glue the cooled sample underneath the label. In this way you will be able to identify each color instantly, and you will have all the information about each color at your fingertips. This simple test sample, if you make it a habit, will save you hours of indecision, tedious work and the grief of spoiling a piece with the wrong color. Later on, you may want to expand each little test sample to include a color's look under different circumstances (fired on metal, over white, over clear flux or silver foil and so on), but this is not necessary at present. Do, however, make a test sample before attempting a major project involving many colors until you become more experienced in the use of enamels and designing with enamel colors. And do not discard the test samples you make for special projects—if you use a copper square, rectangle or disc with a tiny hole for the sample, you will always be able to give your friends handsome enamelled watch fobs, pins or pendants by simply adding a jump ring and a chain.

This set of coasters was slightly over-fired to achieve a speckled effect over the leaves.

Stencilled Coasters

Materials Checklist

pre-formed copper coasters
small bottles of 80-mesh opaque enamel powders in contrasting colors
clean white paper
absorbent paper, such as smooth-finish paper towelling
camel's-hair brush
scissors or sharp knife

Adhesive Solution (same as on page 18)
Cleaning Materials (same as on page 7)
Firing Materials (same as on page 7)

The stencil technique is simple and striking. Even the most complicated designs are easy to achieve with this method, and are limited only by your imagination. For this project we have selected a stencilled leaf motif, but you can use any design you can create, as long as it is relatively simple. It is always best to choose a simple design when you attempt a new enamelling technique, progressing slowly to more and more advanced designs.

After assembling all the materials needed for this project, begin to follow the basic steps in all enamelling projects: polish the copper surface with emery paper, "clean" it in the vinegar-salt-water solution as you did when making the simple pendant, then polish again, and place the ready-to-enamel coasters on a sheet of immaculate white paper.

APPLYING A BASE COAT

Sprinkle a coating of opaque enamel powder over each coaster, covering the top surface completely and building up the edges as you did when making the pendant. This powder will serve as a base coat, so choose a color which will contrast attractively with the color you have chosen for the design —for example, a blue base with opaque green leaves would be a good choice. When the coasters are evenly coated with enamel, fire them. If your kiln is large enough you can fire them all at the same time, but if it is not, fire one coaster at a time.

MAKING A STENCIL

After the coasters have been fired and while they are cooling, trace the outline of a leaf on a piece of cardboard with pencil. Then, with a pair of scissors or razor blade or very sharp knife, carefully cut the leaf out of the cardboard, avoiding making any unnecessary slits. The stiff cardboard will not adhere to the contours of shaped metal structures, so place the cut-out cardboard leaf on a piece of smooth paper towelling, and trace around it with a pencil. Save both the cut-out cardboard leaf and piece of cardboard from which it was cut. Cut the traced leaf carefully out of the paper towelling. Now you will have a rectangular piece of paper towelling with a leaf-shaped hole in it. This will serve as your working stencil. Attach a small strip of paper to an edge of the stencil with a piece of cellophane tape to serve as a handle for the tweezers which you will use to hold the paper-towel stencil when applying the powdered enamel.

APPLYING A STENCIL DESIGN

Now coat one of the fired and cooled coasters lightly with a thin solution of adhesive, using a camel's-hair brush. Place the cut-out stencil over the adhesive-coated coaster, holding the stencil by its paper handle with tweezers. Hold the stencil firmly against the coaster, but remember to avoid touching with your fingers any part of the metal surface to be enamelled, as your fingers are oily and the powdered enamel will not adhere to any oily surface.

With your other hand, sprinkle opaque enamel (as you did when making the pendant) through the cut-out opening in the stencil until you have an even, fairly thick coating. Before removing the stencil, lightly spray a little water (you can use an old nasal atomizer which is perfectly clean for this) over the surface to further affix the powdered enamel.

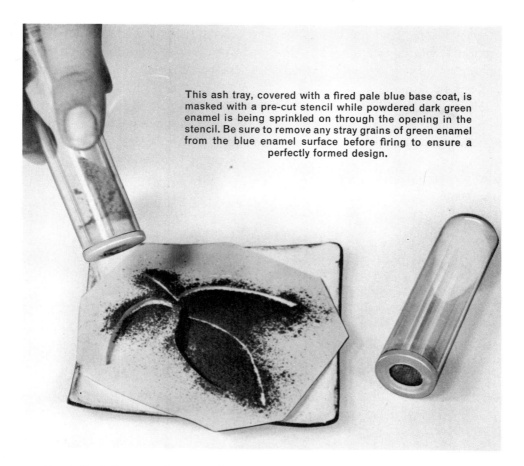

This ash tray, covered with a fired pale blue base coat, is masked with a pre-cut stencil while powdered dark green enamel is being sprinkled on through the opening in the stencil. Be sure to remove any stray grains of green enamel from the blue enamel surface before firing to ensure a perfectly formed design.

Carefully lift away the stencil with your tweezers, and set the coaster aside until the enamel is completely dry before firing it. Since this could take several days in a humid room, you can save time by putting the coaster in an ordinary kitchen oven set at a low temperature for 25 to 30 minutes. When completely dry, fire the coaster in your kiln at 1450° to 1500°F. for 3 minutes.

Follow this procedure with the rest of the coasters. It is wise to work on only one object at a time until you have mastered a technique, or you will find yourself running around your kitchen or work-space frantically, timing pieces being fired, timing pieces drying in the oven, applying the stencil design with one hand on one coaster, and coating still another with adhesive solution. If you do one thing at a time you will discover just how simple and uncomplicated it is to produce original works of art which you will treasure for years to come.

Be sure to save the cardboard leaf pattern stencils, as they can be used again when you enamel other objects in the same motif. You can make new paper-towel stencils if one rips or is damaged. You can also apply a third color with the same cut-out stencil by placing it at another angle on the coaster, or you can vary the color of the design on different coasters using the same stencil.

The leaf design on this bowl was made with the aid of a stencil design. Darker enamel was sprinkled around the edges of the leaf to give it further emphasis.

This design was made by using two stencils and three enamel colors. Another interesting stencil design can be made by sprinkling enamel powder over a previously fired enamel surface through the holes in a delicate paper doily.

Filing

You may find that the edges of your fired pieces have oxidized during the firing process. To remove all traces of oxidation and to polish your enamelled objects, you will need a large and a small metal file, and a carborundum rubbing stone. Use the large file gently to file away oxidation from the edges of your larger fired pieces, the smaller file to file away oxidation from corners, small areas and cloisonné wire. (We will tell you about cloisonné wire later on.) You can give your pieces a smooth finish by polishing them *gently* under cold running water with a carborundum rubbing stone. If you want a glossy effect, rub the filed pieces with a rouge cloth. If you find that an enamelled surface has lost some of its gloss in the first filing, fire it for a few seconds in your kiln at 1300° F. to restore the gloss. *Remove it as soon as it begins to shine.*

If the underside of an object has not been enamelled (as in the first projects) a black scale called *fire scale* will form on the uncoated metal surface during the firing process. To remove this fire scale, drop the cooled object into the "cleaning" solution for a minute or so to loosen the fire scale, and then rub the surface with emery paper to remove any further traces and polish the metal.

A Gay Counter-Enamelled Bowl

Materials Checklist

pre-formed copper bowl, 3 to 4 inches in diameter
small bottle 80-mesh hard-firing opaque enamel in bright color
small bottle 80-mesh hard-firing beige-colored enamel powder
camel's-hair brush
atomizer or sprayer
stilt or firing stand

Adhesive Solution (same as on page 18)
Cleaning Materials (same as on page 7)
Firing Materials (same as on page 7)

When exposed to a great heat, as in the kiln firing process, copper expands to a much greater degree than enamel. Correspondingly, during the cooling process, copper contracts to a much greater degree than the fired enamel coating. This expansion-contraction process puts enormous stress on the copper (the larger the object, the greater the stress is), and causes warping and cracking of the enamel surface. This is especially unfortunate when an enamelled design has been created on the surface of a piece, since the design will almost invariably become misshapen and even destroyed. So it is necessary to coat most pieces on both sides with enamel, thus "sealing" the metal and reinforcing it. In this way, most warping and cracking is avoided. If you are ever in doubt as to whether or not you should counter-enamel a piece, play it safe and do so. Even such tiny objects as cuff links, earrings and pendants benefit from counter-enamelling.

There are various ways to counter-enamel, and we will explain the two preferred methods. After experimenting with each, you can decide which is easier and more comfortable for you. Each has its advantages and disadvantages, so it is really a matter of personal preference.

This deep bowl was enamelled on both sides in a rich cherry-red opaque enamel. The tiny holes in the middle resulted from a slight over-firing, and because red enamels tend to burn away quickly.

Remember that the word "counter-enamel" refers to the enamel coating on the back of an enamelled object, and always use a hard-firing enamel for this back coating.

SIMULTANEOUS COUNTER-ENAMELLING

Although it is possible to enamel the back of an object, fire it, and then enamel the top side, you will save much time and tedious work by learning to enamel both sides of an object at the same time. Simultaneous counter-enamelling is tricky but not difficult, and care and patience will produce a perfect result every time.

Before you begin to enamel, polish the small copper bowl with emery paper and "clean" it as you cleaned the simple pendant. With a pair of clean tweezers, place the bowl on a sheet of immaculate white paper. Always remember to avoid touching, with your fingers, the metal surface to be enamelled. To make it easier to obtain an even coating of powdered enamel on the curved sides of the bowl, first "paint" the inside of the bowl with adhesive using a camel's-hair brush. Apply the adhesive coat lightly, evenly and thinly.

Then sprinkle on a coat of brightly colored enamel (sunny yellow, vibrant emerald green or peacock blue would be good choices since they are brilliant and hard-firing) as you did when making the simple pendant. When the inside of the bowl is thoroughly and evenly coated, *lightly* spray a *little* adhesive over the powdered enamel surface to further affix the enamel powder to the metal.

Place a stilt or firing stand in a convenient place near the kitchen oven where the bowl is to be dried before firing. (You can improvise such a stand by bending a rectangular piece of tin up at each of its four edges.) Then, *gently*, grasp the bowl by its very edges and invert it over the firing stand. To do this you will have to touch the bowl with your fingers, so to minimize the damage that this will cause, wet your fingers in the vinegar-salt-water cleaning solution, to remove the surface skin oil. Dry them with an immaculate white cloth before touching the bowl. When the bowl is inverted on the firing stand, resting on the supports by its edges, lightly brush the areas your fingers touched with a damp—not soaking wet!—piece of paper towelling moistened in the cleaning solution. Be sure to remove all traces of oil on the back of the bowl. This is the "tricky" step in simultaneous counter-enamelling, but if you proceed calmly and carefully you will have no problem.

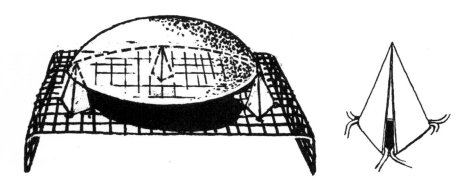

You can improvise a firing stand by bending three pieces of tin into little pyramids (right) and wiring them to a steel mesh stand. The bowl is then inverted over the pyramids.

This counter-enamelled bowl is ready to be fired on a professional stilt wired to a steel mesh planch. Since the bowl has curved edges, it is fired right side up, but any object without curved edges must be fired upside down to minimize stilt marks and damage to the enamel surface.

The bowl will remain upside down from this point on until it is fired and cooled. You will enamel the back of the bowl just as you enamelled the inside: Brush a coat of adhesive over the whole surface of the back, lightly and evenly, and sprinkle on a coat of hard-firing beige enamel. When the back is evenly coated, spray the powdered enamel surface lightly with adhesive. Slide your enamelling fork or spatula under the firing stand, and transfer it carefully, the bowl and all, to the oven which has been set at a low temperature. There the bowl will dry before it is fired. All the water should evaporate in 20 to 25 minutes.

Unless you use the oven, it might take several days for all the water to evaporate in a humid room. If you fire the bowl before it is dry, the water in the adhesive solution will boil under the stress of the high firing temperature and ruin the enamel coating. It is also possible to "dry" the bowl by placing it in a hot kiln for 3 seconds and removing it instantly, but this is a risky and dangerous procedure, especially when you are working with children. If you dry the bowl in the kiln a little cloud of steam will form around it as you remove it from the kiln. This cloud of steam is the evaporated water escaping into the air.

When the bowl is dry, slide your enamelling fork or spatula under the firing stand again, and transfer it all to the kiln. Fire the bowl at 1450°F. for about 2 minutes, or until the enamel reaches the "wavy" stage. This is called under-firing enamel. Always under-fire a counter-enamelled object the first time, or you will not be able to fire it again. Remember that counter-enamelling is the first *stage* in most enamelling projects. Plain or solid color enamel objects will require at least 3 firings, and designed and detailed objects will require as many as 8 or 9 firings before they are completed. So if you fire the first enamel coat until it is hard and glossy it will not withstand successive firings, and will probably crack open, spoiling the piece.

After the bowl has cooled you can touch up any imperfections, such as tiny marks from the firing stand, bubbles, or blemishes, with powdered enamel (remember to use the right color on the right side) and fire the bowl again. Do not remove the bowl from its firing stand until it is completely cool, or you will damage the enamel. During the last firing, allow the enamel to reach the hard, glossy stage. This will happen when the temperature inside the kiln reaches 1600°F.

When your bowl has cooled after the final firing you will have a beautifully simple example of the rich colors enamel alone achieves, and you will have learned perhaps the most important technique in successful enamelling.

COUNTER-ENAMELLING ONE SIDE AT A TIME

A recent development in the field of enamelling has simplified the once tedious procedure of enamelling one side of an object at a time. Unprotected metal surfaces will form black flakes called *fire scale* during the firing process. This fire scale must be completely removed before enamel can be applied to a metal surface, and the area must be cleaned and pickled all over again. So, in the past, it was preferable to enamel both sides of an object at a time, to avoid the tedious dual cleaning, pickling, polishing and enamelling process. Now enamel suppliers offer a product that is simply brushed on the top side of the object, and allowed to dry. Then enamel is sprinkled on the back of the "clean" object and under-fired as usual. During the cooling process the protective coating on the top side scales off, leaving the surface perfectly clean and ready to enamel. This technique eliminates the delicate "turning" in simultaneous counter-enamelling, though it is essentially the same in every other way.

Your "surprise" ash tray might look like this. Here the lumps were allowed to melt almost completely, and as they melted they flowed down the sides of the ash tray in an interesting pattern. Lumps of enamel were allowed to melt and flow down the sides of the previously fired dark blue ash tray on the right.

A "Surprise" Textured Ash Tray

Materials Checklist

pre-formed copper ash tray with a bowl shape
80-mesh hard-firing opaque enamel in a light color
soft-firing enamel lumps, various bright colors
tweezers

Adhesive Solution (as before)

Cleaning Materials (as before)

Firing Materials (as before)

As explained on page 24, there are soft-, medium- and hard-firing enamels. Soft enamels melt at a lower temperature than medium and hard enamels, and by taking advantage of this you can achieve strikingly unique decorative effects. By interrupting the firing process when the lumps are half-melted you will obtain a three-dimensional effect.

Before you begin, clean and polish the ash tray as you have done in the previous projects. The ash tray will need a light-colored base coat to contrast with the brightly colored lumps, so enamel the ash tray on both sides in a hard-firing beige, white, or grey opaque enamel, as you did when making the counter-enamelled bowl. Remember to *under-fire* the ash tray so that it will withstand several firings. You may have to apply 2 or 3 coats of enamel before it is even and smooth.

When the ash tray is evenly enamelled with the base coat, fired and cool, coat the edges lightly with adhesive solution, so that the lumps will adhere to

Eight rows of transparent enamel lumps were perched on this previously enamelled candleholder and held in place by adhesive while they were being applied. The candleholder was thoroughly dried before it was fired. Near the middle of the candleholder the lumps remained stationary, and so almost retained their original shape, while near the top edge of the candleholder the lumps melted and flowed down the steep sides. The cloisonné technique was used to achieve the abstract effect of the cuff links on the right.

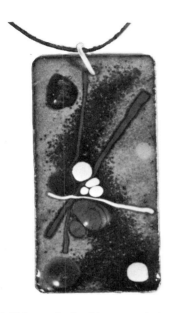

(Left) This pendant achieves an abstract appearance through the imaginative use of lumps and threads. (Right) The lid of the canister was first enamelled with an opaque white base coat, and then decorated with enamel lumps and threads and re-fired.

the surface. You will find that each lump has a tiny flat base to balance on. Using a pair of clean tweezers, pick up the lumps one by one and perch them around the adhesive-coated rim of the ash tray, resting the lumps on their tiny bases. If you find that some of them fall off, apply a little more adhesive to that area. Another thing to remember is that the larger the lumps, the likelier it is that they will pop off after they are fired, so use the smallest lumps in your assortment. When all the lumps are in place around the rim of the ash tray, spray them lightly with adhesive solution and put the ash tray aside to dry. (Remember that whenever you use an adhesive solution or any moist property in enamelling you must dry the wet enamel surface before it is fired or the piece will be ruined.)

When the ash tray is dry, fire it at 1400°F. for about 1½ minutes, or until the little lumps begin to melt and slide down the sides of the ash tray. If

Lumps and threads were placed on previously fired bracelet links to create an appearance resembling cloisonné.

you fire it longer, the lumps will melt completely, and will dissolve into the base coat. Thus, the three-dimensional effect you are trying to achieve will be lost.

The colors you choose, the position of the lumps on the ash tray, and the heat and length of the firing time will be slightly different in every case, so it would be impossible to predict just what the finished ash tray will look like. Since the hard-firing base coat will not be effected by the 1400°F. temperature required to melt the soft-firing lumps, which will half-melt and slide down the walls of the ash tray, you will achieve a textured, semi-striped effect, which will be unique and a surprise in the bargain!

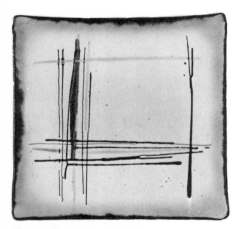 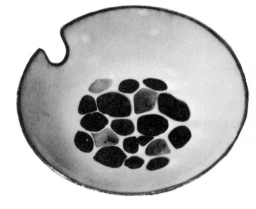

(Right) Tiny enamel lumps were half-melted on a previously fired beige enamel base coat to create this pebbled ash tray. (Left) Lumps and threads were used here to create still more unusual designs. The square ash tray was covered with a white enamel base coat and fired. Then enamel threads were placed in a square pattern and the tray was fired again. The thin threads melted into rather thick lines, while thicker threads retained their original shape.

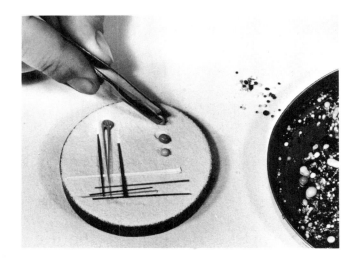

Enamel lumps and threads are placed in a pleasing pattern on top of an unfired enamel-coated disc. By firing the base coat and decorations together, an irregularly veined look will be achieved, as the lumps melt into the base coating.

This technique is especially suited to objects with curved, steep walls and sides such as bowls, dishes and cups. You can form a pattern with the lumps before firing, use lumps of a single color, or combine lumps and threads for an endless variety of creative decorations.

A combination of lumps and threads were placed on this previously fired white enamel square dish. They were barely allowed to fuse to the surface, retaining their original shape, and showing a bas-relief effect.

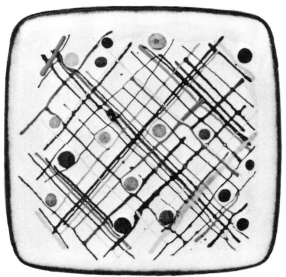

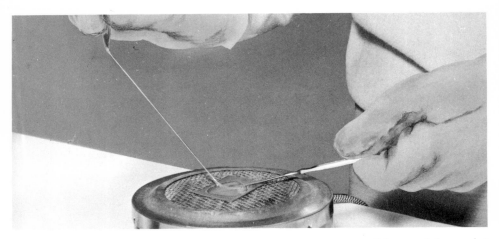

(Below) This is how the match-box cover and bracelet were made: small heaps of dry enamel powder were placed on a previously fired enamel surface, and the objects were re-fired. The heaps of enamel powder were allowed to burn into the base coating, and they were quickly pulled apart with the tool pictured on top. (Children should not attempt to do this, as they might be burned.) (Above) Enamel threads can be made by melting enamel and forming long threads. The threads will cool almost immediately, and will break off if you tug them slightly. Put each thread on a clean piece of paper nearby as you work, and store the finished threads in a clean glass jar.

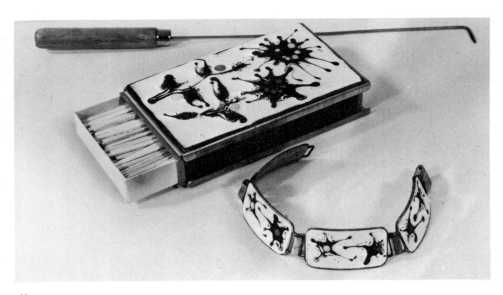

This is how your dark green flowered pen-and-pencil tray will look. This floral design would also look pretty on a powder box.

A Flowered Pen-and-Pencil Tray

Materials Checklist

pre-formed copper tray, about $2\frac{1}{2}$ inches wide by 6 inches long
80-mesh hard-firing enamel powder, dark color
tiny enamel lumps and threads, white, yellow and green

Adhesive Solution (as before)

Cleaning Materials (as before)

Firing Materials (as before)

An attractive gift for special friends is a three-dimensional flowered pen-and-pencil tray. Instead of allowing the lumps to half-melt as you did when making the "surprise" ash tray, you can achieve a relief effect by firing them just long enough to fuse them to a previously fired enamel surface. If your kiln is too small for a tray 6 inches long, you can use a small square ash tray form and give it as a paper clip holder.

Clean and polish the copper tray. When it is ready to enamel, place it on a piece of immaculate white paper. It must be counter-enamelled, so you can either enamel the underside of the tray in the same color, or, since the tray is flat, and the underside will not show, you can use *commercial counter-enamel*. Suppliers offer an enamel which is made up of hard-firing scrap enamel—a conglomeration of opaque and/or transparent enamel. Commercial counter-enamel is cheaper than enamel powder meant for top coatings, but you will not save a great deal of money unless you do large quantities of counter-enamelling as professionals do. It is good to know about commercial counter-enamel, however, so experiment with it on flat objects when a back coating is needed but will not show.

Since the lump and thread decoration will be fired only briefly, fire the tray almost completely at 1500°F. during the counter-enamelling process. It should almost reach the glossy stage.

When the tray is cool, you can begin to apply the flower design. Sketch the outlines of the tray on a piece of white paper in order to plan the arrangement of flowers, or arrange them as in the illustration above. Moisten a camel's-hair brush with adhesive solution, and lightly brush a little adhesive on the tiny base of each lump as you put it in place on the tray. We used white lumps for the flower petals, and tiny yellow lumps for the "eyes." Then place green enamel threads and green enamel lumps to form the stems and leaves of the flowers. When all the pieces are in place, fire the tray briefly at a high (1500-1550°F.) temperature. Fire the tray only until the bases of the lumps and threads melt and adhere to the base coating, or the design will be spoiled. The firing time will vary, but one minute or a little more should be about right. It is better to under-fire a design like this than to over-fire it.

After the tray is cool you can file away any oxidation around its edges for a more finished look. This little tray, so simple to make, is ideal for children to make for special gift-giving occasions.

A Luminous Leaf Brooch

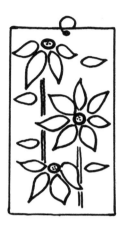

Materials Checklist

   pre-formed copper brooch
   camel's-hair brush
   80-mesh dark green opaque enamel powder
   80-mesh pale green transparent enamel powder

Adhesive Solution (as before)

Cleaning Materials (as before)

Firing Materials (as before)

Several techniques are available for achieving designs in enamel, and each technique has its own effect on the design you create. The leaves you applied on coasters with the stencil technique will look quite different if applied "free-hand." In this project, you will do this by "painting" leaves on an enamelled background with adhesive, and dusting enamel powder over the "painted" wet surface, in the following manner:

Before you can begin to paint on the design, you must counter-enamel the brooch in a background color. (We used dark green opaque enamel.) You can use a single color for both sides, or you can enamel the back of the brooch in a contrasting color. One color is easier to work with, however, and since the back of the brooch will not show, it is not necessary to spend a great deal of extra time and effort enamelling the back in a different color. Clean, polish, sprinkle and fire the brooch 2 or 3 times as you did when making the counter-enamelled bowl. During the last firing, allow the enamel to reach the glossy stage briefly, and cool the brooch.

45

1. Paint . . .   2. shake . . .   3. tap.

Now "paint" a leaf on the cooled brooch, using a camel's-hair brush and a medium-thick adhesive solution. First outline the leaf, and then fill it in. Make the leaf as simple as possible, because fine lines and angles will be lost during the firing process. (If the adhesive seems to "creep," moisten a piece of paper towelling with saliva or vinegar and light brush this over the surface of the enamelled brooch. Now the adhesive will adhere to the enamelled surface.)

Sprinkle a coating of pale green transparent enamel powder over the adhesive-coated area. When the area is evenly coated with enamel, carefully lift the brooch and tap it lightly against the table you are working on. The enamel powder will adhere to the adhesive-coated leaf design, and will fall away from the uncoated area. Use a clean camel's-hair brush to remove any stray grains of enamel.

The brooch must be dried before you can fire it, so either put it in a kitchen oven set at a low temperature for 25 to 30 minutes, or hold the pendant on the enamelling fork (remember to wear asbestos gloves) outside the open kiln door until it stops smoking. (The smoke is simply the oil in the adhesive burning away.)

Fire the brooch at 1550°F. for 2 to 4 minutes, or until the surface is glossy. When it is cool, examine the leaf design to see if it is smooth and even. If not, sprinkle enamel on the imperfect areas and fire the brooch again.

If you hear a cracking sound while the brooch (or any enamelled object for that matter) is in the kiln, leave it in the kiln until the enamel melts completely and heals the cracks which have appeared. Most pieces will "crack" during the firing process as the metal expands under the influence of extreme heat, but the cracks will heal if your pieces are fired long enough at the proper temperature.

When your brooch is cool, choose a catch or fastener from your selection of "findings," and glue or solder it (we will tell you how to solder later on) to the back of the brooch. Following this same technique, you can make a pair of earrings with a leaf design to match your brooch. The transparent pale green enamel you used for the leaf design will give a mysterious glow to the brooch and earrings under electric or candle light, so they will be especially effective to wear at night.

As you have learned by now, the basic enamelling techniques are not difficult in themselves. What you must concentrate on is *how to apply* these techniques. By comparing the brooch you have just made with the stencilled coasters, you can see how each technique reacts to the same design. The stencilled leaf will look more precise, and will contrast more with its background. The "painted" leaf will not be so precisely defined, and will blend subtly with its background. This visual comparison will help you achieve a *working knowledge* of each technique, so that when you create your own designs you will be able to choose the technique that will enhance them most.

Several shades of red enamel were applied to the links of this bracelet with the "wet inlay" technique. Each shade was mixed with distilled water, applied separately and pushed into position with a spreader, dried and fired. This method produces extremely rich color tones, but is very difficult and should be attempted only by experts.

(Left) A treasured example of the Ch'ien Lung period is this breathtakingly beautiful cloisonné figure of a woman. It is three feet high, and one of a pair made in China about A.D. 1720.

(Right) Another example of a simple cloisonné design is this delightful red dish with blue and yellow cloisonné railway cars. Although cloisonné "cells" traditionally are filled with enamel to create color separation, an interesting variation is this green brooch, with the wire cells left empty, accented with glass "jewels." The link bracelet was decorated with red and blue flowers on an opaque white enamel background, using the Limoges (fine brush-work enamel painting) technique.

A Picturesque Veined Nut Dish

Materials Checklist

pre-formed copper dish with curved sides
80-mesh *soft-firing* enamel powder
80-mesh *hard-firing* enamel powder

Cleaning Materials (as before)
Adhesive Solution (as before)
Firing Materials (as before)

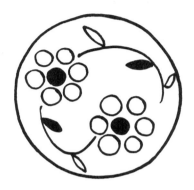

By firing a hard enamel on top of a soft enamel you can obtain a spotty, veined pattern. This is most effective when the colors used contrast sharply with each other. As long as the coatings become progressively harder (in other words, the bottom coating is the softest firing, the next a little harder-firing, the next a medium-firing and the top coating a hard-firing enamel) you can fire as many as 4 colors on top of each other. As the soft-firing enamels bubble up through the harder-firing enamels during the firing process, all the colors will be exposed in an irregular, abstract pattern.

Before you begin, clean and polish the dish, and place it on a piece of immaculate white paper. Since the dish is to be fired several times and the first coat on the top side must be of soft-firing enamel, it is essential to counter-enamel the dish with an extremely hard-firing enamel, so that it will withstand the pressures of many firings and several coatings of enamel. If you neglect this step the counter-enamel will not be able to withstand the pressure of the metal expansion and will crack, so you must choose a hard-firing color such as beige for the back of the dish, and a soft-firing enamel such as white, red, black or even clear transparent ("flux") enamel for the top side. Apply the enamel to both sides as you did when making the counter-enamelled bowl (see page 32) and fire the dish at 1400° to 1450°F. for about 3 minutes, or until it reaches the wavy stage.

When the dish is cool, sprinkle a coat of hard-firing enamel in a sharply contrasting color on the top side of the dish. (If you want to apply 3 colors, this second sprinkling should be a *medium-firing* enamel.) If the dish is going to be fired again, do not allow it to reach the glossy stage, but remove it from the kiln when it reaches the wavy stage. After the dish is cool, sprinkle on a third contrasting color of extremely hard-firing enamel, and fire the dish again until it reaches the glossy stage (4 minutes at 1550° to 1600°F.) and the soft enamel has bubbled up through the hard enamel.

Textures resulting from this technique can rarely be pre-determined, but as you become more experienced you will be able to calculate the approximate end-result. It is fun to use techniques such as this for their beauty and excitement, but as you progress in enamelling try not to depend solely on "surprise" effects. You will achieve greater individuality and satisfaction by venturing your skill on your own designs, and adapting these techniques to them. For example, you can incorporate this "over-firing" technique into a design of your own by applying the soft enamel on *restricted* areas of an object, firing it, and then covering the object completely with a coat of hard-firing enamel. The veined pattern will appear only in the areas you covered with soft-firing enamel.

By using your imagination to adapt the techniques you have learned to your own designs, you will be on your way to becoming a true craftsman.

The little sailing boats on the bracelet links are the result of an enamel thread decoration, and they somewhat resemble the effect of champlevé (see page 98).

(Above) This fish-shaped dish was covered with an opaque red base coat. After it was fired and cooled, black enamel powder was mixed with a little bit of distilled water and the lines were painted on with a camel's-hair brush. The dish was thoroughly dried before it was re-fired at 1500° F. for three minutes. (Left) A heavy, solid block of copper was coated with little heaps of enamel, which ran down the sides during the intense firing process, giving the block a three-dimensional, glossy appearance. This cube would make an unusual paperweight.

"Professional" Abstract Cuff Links

Materials Checklist

pre-formed copper cuff links
80-mesh enamel powders in contrasting colors
clean white paper

Firing Materials (as before)
Acid Cleaning Solution (see below)

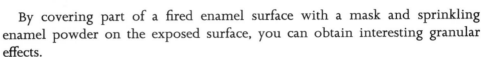

By covering part of a fired enamel surface with a mask and sprinkling enamel powder on the exposed surface, you can obtain interesting granular effects.

The "masking" technique is simple and dramatic, so it looks best when applied in 2, or at most 3, colors. You will achieve the most effective 2-color designs by choosing colors which are particularly attractive side by side, or by using a lighter shade of a single color in transparent enamel over opaque enamel. Black-and-white, blue-and-green, red-and-orange, transparent blue-on-opaque-blue, and transparent green-on-opaque-green are only a few of the combinations which are especially suitable for 2-color designs. Before we begin, however, we will discuss a more professional way to clean metal objects to be enamelled.

HOW TO CLEAN METAL WITH ACID

Up to now you have cleaned objects to be enamelled by "pickling" them in a vinegar-salt-water solution. Vinegar is an effective substitute for the more common acid solution used by professionals, and is recommended if you are working with children. Acid, however, will do a more thorough job of cleaning, and is preferred to vinegar for a more professional, or finished, look.

The traditional concentrated nitric acid solution has many serious drawbacks, all of which have been overcome by a new, inexpensive, and, more important, perfectly safe, dry acid compound for pickling, sold under various trade names. To use it, simply mix 1 tablespoon of the dry acid compound

The pair of cuff links on the upper left were made with the champlevé technique (see page 98), while the rest were made in cloisonné (see page 87). As you can see by comparing the cuff links, champlevé produces a color separation that is much less defined than cloisonné.

to each cup of water in a large glass container. Warm the object to be cleaned for 10 seconds in your kiln, immerse the warm metal in the solution with your tongs, swish it around, and then remove it. After a thorough rinsing with water, the metal will be perfectly clean and ready to enamel. The method is very simple, and the solution is so stable it can be used over and over again.

Concentrated nitric acid mixed with water is the traditional method of cleaning metal. In case you are unable to obtain the dry acid compound for pickling, you will have to use it. Before mixing the nitric acid solution, several steps are necessary:

To burn away oil, impurities and grease, heat the metal to be enamelled— cuff links in this case—in your kiln or over a burner to a dull red color. If you heat the metal too long, too much fire scale will form, and it will be difficult to remove. Cool the metal (if you drop it in the acid solution before it is cool, it may warp) while you are preparing the acid pickling solution.

Since the acid solution is strong and potentially dangerous, select a heat-resistant glass or procelain container with a tight-fitting lid to mix and store the solution. Choose a container which is large enough to accommodate the objects you will clean in it.

The next step is to mix the acid solution. Some professionals use a solution of 1 part concentrated nitric acid to 2 parts water, but this solution is not recommended for beginners. A solution of 1 part of concentrated nitric acid to 5 parts water is more than adequate. Before you mix the acid and the water together remember to

always add the acid to the water.

By adding the acid to the water you prevent violent spattering and possible harm to yourself. Also

never add a hot metal object to the acid solution

for this, too, could be dangerous. If you follow these rules and remember to keep the acid covered while it is not in use, you will be safe at all times. Cleaning metal with acid is really easier and more satisfactory than cleaning it in vinegar, salt and water, if you follow this safe, simple procedure:

Place the water in the glass or porcelain container which you have chosen. Add 1 part of acid for every 5 parts of water (in other words, if you use 5 cups of water add 1 cup of acid). Be sure that the container is no more than half full, so the solution will not run over. Using a pair of tongs, stir the acid and water gently until they are mixed.

Then lower the cooled cuff links into the acid solution with your tongs. Leave them in the solution until all the fire scale has disappeared and their surface is pink and clean. Stir the acid solution from time to time to prevent the acid from eating around portions of the fire scale still on the cuff links, which would cause an uneven surface. When the cuff links are clean, remove them one at a time with your tongs, and rinse them well under cold running water. When they are thoroughly rinsed, dry them with a lint-free, clean cloth to prevent brown stains from forming as the water evaporates.

Since you are going to cover the surface of the cuff links with opaque enamel, no further polishing is necessary. When transparent enamels are going to be used, allowing the copper to show through, polish the copper surface a little more with fine steel wool. As the steel wool may leave some grease, wipe the surface with a little detergent mixed with water and dry

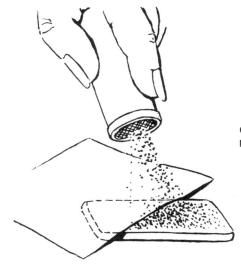

Cover part of the previously fired cuff link with a paper "mask" and sprinkle enamel over the exposed area.

thoroughly. Keep and use steel wool away from your enamel powders, for if particles of steel wool get into the powders (a little breeze will do it) they will show up as "fish hooks" in the fired enamel coating. Another suggestion: do not clean metal objects too far in advance or they may become dirty and greasy again.

The final step before applying the enamel is to remove the acid, making the surface alkaline, to facilitate enamelling. Wipe the cuff links with a clean piece of paper towelling moistened in saliva, household ammonia, or a detergent. (Use neither tap water nor ordinary soap as it contains grease.)

ENAMELLING ON AN ACID-CLEANED SURFACE

There is absolutely no difference in procedure when you enamel on an acid-clean surface. The only difference is the final look of your enamel creations. They will be shinier, smoother, and more professionally "finished."

Sprinkle a base coat of opaque enamel on the cuff links. Counter-enamel them in the same color and fire them. When they are fired and cool (remember, you may have to sprinkle and fire them 2 or 3 times before they are even and smooth), place them on a piece of immaculate white paper.

Using another piece of immaculate white paper as a mask, cover part of one of the cuff links, and sprinkle enamel in a contrasting color over the exposed portion of the cuff link. Cover half of the cuff link, or cover a corner of the cuff link, or whatever part you want to leave free of the second color to be applied.

This is a good time to try "designing." When you have an even layer of enamel on the exposed portion of the cuff link, slowly remove the paper mask you held over part of the cuff link. You can obtain an interesting effect by tilting the mask slightly, so that the extra grains of enamel which fell on the mask during the sprinkling process slide off the mask and on to the previously covered portion of the cuff link. When the cuff link is fired, these grains of enamel will look like a tiny comet's tail trailing off the cuff link.

Sprinkle the other cuff link in the same way, and fire them together in your kiln at 1500-1550°F. (if you used soft-firing enamel for the second color, fire at 1450°F.) for 2 to 4 minutes. When the cuff links are cool, sprinkle and fire them again if necessary. If you would like an even more colorful effect, hold the paper mask over each cuff link at a different angle and sprinkle on still a third color. Sprinkle the third color on lightly though, for if you have too many enamel layers the counter-enamel will not withstand the strain and will crack.

When the cuff links are completely cool, file away their rough edges and polish them under cold running water with your carborundum rubbing stone. Glue or solder fasteners from your selection of findings on the backs of the cuff links.

HOW TO STORE YOUR ACID CLEANING SOLUTION

Store your acid cleaning solution in a safe, dry place, away from children. In time it will turn blue from the dissolved copper, so when it turns a deep blue, is filled with pieces of fire scale, or if brown fumes rise from it, discard it and prepare a new solution. If copper pieces being cleaned develop a spotted surface, the acid solution is too strong, and must be diluted. To do this, pour some water into a second container, and add the acid solution to this, so as not to violate the cardinal rule when working with acid: always to add acid to water.

The pre-formed copper bracelet must be dis-assembled before enamel-ling. Large squares like these are especially suited to the sgraffito technique, as fine lines would be "lost" on smaller squares.

A "Scratched" Link Bracelet

Materials Checklist

pre-formed copper link bracelet
80-mesh hard-firing opaque enamel, dark color
80-mesh opaque enamel powder, light color
sharp, pointed tool such as a steel knitting needle or tiny letter opener

Cleaning Materials (as before)

Firing Materials (as before)

The "scratching" technique, called sgraffito, is simply the scratching of a design through an unfired layer of enamel to reach a previously fired enamel layer in a sharply contrasting color underneath. For example, it you place a white piece of paper over a black piece of paper, and then cut the outline of a shape (a flower, a box, anything) out of the white paper, the black paper under-neath will show through the openings you have cut. By using a sharply pointed tool (professionals use a jeweler's scribe) to scratch lines in an unfired coating of enamel powder over a fired coating, the coating underneath is exposed. This is how to do it:

First of all, disassemble the bracelet so you have a series of links. Counter-enamel each link in a single, hard-firing dark color. When the links are all fired and cool, place them on a sheet of immaculate white paper. Work on one link at a time from this point on.

Sprinkle a link with light colored opaque enamel powder. When it is evenly coated, scratch a design through the powdered enamel with a sharp

1. The bracelet link is covered with dark colored enamel, fired and cooled. 2. The bracelet link is then covered with light colored enamel powder. 3. A design is scratched through the unfired enamel coating with a sharp pointed tool such as a knitting needle. Then the bracelet link is fired again.

1

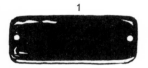

2

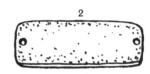

3

tool, such as a knitting needle. You can draw a tree, or form a pyramid of little lines, for example. Then fire the link at 1550°F. for 2 to 4 minutes, or until it is smooth and glossy. When it is cool, examine it to see if your design shows clearly. If not, your lines were too thin. You can remedy this by sifting another coat of transparent enamel over the link, scratching the design again with a thicker tool, and firing it again. Experiment with this first link until you are satisfied with the way it looks. Then repeat the process with each link. When all the links are fired and cool, re-assemble the links. Fasten the little rings holding the links together with your round-nosed pliers.

You can further embellish an sgraffito design by "painting" dark-colored enamel lines over the fired design. To do this, mix the enamel powder you used as a base coating with a little adhesive solution, and paint the lines on with a camel's-hair brush. (Do not forget to dry the enamel before firing it if you do this.) When the enamel is dry, fire the object again. The painted lines will be much heavier and darker than the scratched lines.

Remember that the 2 layers must be contrasting colors. If the base coating is dark, the top coating must be light in color. If the base coating is light, the top coating must be dark. And the design is scratched through *unfired* enamel on top of a contrasting *fired* enamel coating. (Although you can also sift powdered enamel right over a clean, bare copper surface and scratch to expose the metal surface itself, this would require counter-enamelling on the underside first and re-cleaning of the top side, so this is not recommended for beginners.)

Another interesting design can be obtained by "scratching" the design with an ordinary pocket comb. This will produce a series of parallel lines.

A Pair of Geometric Earrings

Materials Checklist

pre-formed copper earrings
80-mesh transparent and opaque enamel powders
small piece of solder
earring backs (findings)

Cleaning Materials (as before)
Firing Materials (as before)

Enamelling is such a flexible art that there are an infinite number of ways to achieve varying designs. You have learned several ways to apply enamel powders to metal surfaces to obtain designs, and you have begun to venture your skill in composing your own designs. By now you are beginning to achieve a certain amount of skill in enamelling, and you will want to "finish" your creations as professionally as possible. In this project we will show you still another way to make a design with a dry enamel powder over a fired enamel base coat, and we will also tell you how to solder, so that your jewelry creations will be enduring and professional-looking.

Clean and polish each copper earring. Counter-enamel each (on both sides) in a single, opaque enamel color. *Leave a tiny area free of enamel on the back of each*

1. The earring is covered with enamel and fired.
2. After the earring is cool, enamel powder in a contrasting color is sprinkled on.
3. Parts of the unfired contrasting enamel coating are brushed away, exposing the fired layer underneath, and forming a design.

earring, where the findings will be soldered on later. Solder will not adhere to an enamelled surface. When they are fired and cool, begin to apply a "dry brush" design in the following manner:

Place the enamelled earrings on a sheet of immaculate white paper. Moisten a piece of paper towelling in saliva, vinegar or household ammonia, and lightly brush the paper towelling over the top surface of the earrings to make the surface alkaline. Let the moisture dry before applying the enamel powder. When the surface to be enamelled is dry, sprinkle on a coat of transparent enamel, completely covering the surface. Now, using a clean, dry brush, brush *away* areas of the powdered enamel to form a design by exposing the enamel coating underneath. The best designs to form with this technique are geometric forms, such as semi-circles, squares, and triangles. Tiny forms and angles will not survive the firing process, but will melt into a formless shape, so strive for a simple, rather large and striking design. The base color will show where you have brushed the top layer away, so be sure to use colors which look pretty together (such as black and white, or 2 shades of the same color).

Fire the earrings until they are smooth and glossy. When they are completely cool, you can file and polish the edges and top surface with your carborundum rubbing stone. If any of the gloss is lost during this process, fire the earrings again at 1350°F. for about 30 seconds, or until they just begin to shine in the kiln. When they are cool, you can complete them with backs from your selection of findings.

HOW TO SOLDER

Soldering is really very simple. All you have to remember are two things: all soldering must be done *after* an object is enamelled, and the surface to be soldered must be *absolutely clean*, so always brush the surface with a little detergent or ammonia before applying solder, and make sure it is free of tiny bits of fire scale.

Lay the earrings, with the top side down, on top of your kiln. (If you are firing with a Bunsen burner, lay the earrings on the lower plate, top side down.) The kiln should be warm but not hot. In other words, unplug the kiln after

A soldered cuff link is being removed from the kiln as soon as the solder has flowed (melted), to prevent damage to the enamelled surface.

you fire the earrings, and by the time the earrings are cool the kiln should be barely warm to the touch outside. (If you are using a Bunsen burner do not turn it on yet.) Next lay an earring back (a finding) on one of the earrings, over the hole you left unenamelled for this purpose.

You will probably discover that solder is available in little tubes similar to tooth-paste tubes, though it sometimes comes packaged in other ways. If it comes in a tube, squeeze $\frac{1}{8}$ inch of solder out of the tube and place it right next to the finding on the back of the earring. (For larger objects—such as brooches—use $\frac{1}{4}$ inch of solder.) If the solder comes in a jar, box or roll, take a small amount of solder out of its container (or unroll it) with a small stick or spatula, and place it on the earring-back next to the finding. The solder will be easy to handle if you cut it with scissors or even a razor blade.

Follow the same procedure for the other earring. *After the solder and parts are in place on the earrings, plug in the kiln (or turn on the lower Bunsen or butane burner). The solder will melt and flow around the finding as the kiln (or burner) heats. As soon as the solder has melted and "flowed"* remove the earrings with your long tweezers or enamelling fork and turn off the kiln (or burner). If you leave the earrings on the kiln after the solder has melted and flowed the enamelled surface will be damaged.

Your earrings should look just as "finished" and professional—and even more original—as any jewelry for sale today!

69

A Golden Crackle Plate

Materials Checklist

pre-formed copper dish, 4 to 5 inches in diameter, fairly flat shape
80-mesh soft-firing black enamel powder
80-mesh hard-firing black enamel powder
80-mesh red transparent enamel powder
gold liquid metallic lustre
camel's-hair brush
carbon tetrachloride (lighter fluid)
paper towelling

Adhesive Solution (as before)

Cleaning Materials (as before)

Firing Materials (as before)

The use of liquid metallic lustres has produced some of the most beautiful enamelled objects in the world. The crackle effect we are seeking in this project is obtained by over-firing gold metallic lustre, which is a solution of metallic salts dissolved in oil.

Do not confuse liquid metallic *lustres* with liquid *metals*, which are, as the name implies, precious metals (gold, palladium or platinum) suspended with metallic resinates in solution. Liquid metals are far more expensive than liquid metallic lustres, and are not really within the scope of a beginner. Liquid metallic lustres give such handsome results and are so much easier to work with that you will be more than satisfied to confine yourself to working with them at present.

The copper surface must be especially clean for this technique, so it is preferable to use the acid cleaning solution, rather than the vinegar solution. After it is polished and perfectly clean, enamel the back of the dish in a hard-firing black enamel, and the front of the dish in a soft-firing enamel. This step is extremely important, for if you use a soft-firing enamel on the back it will

The top of this wooden box was decorated with enamel brush-work. Light brown, yellow and green 200-mesh enamel powders were each mixed with Indian sandalwood oil, and the flower was "painted" on a previously fired enamel base with the wet enamel pap, using a camel's-hair brush and a spreader for larger areas. The lid was thoroughly dried before it was fired. This is the "Limoges" application, and since it requires great skill, wait until you are experienced before attempting it.

crack, and if you use a hard-firing enamel on the front it will spoil the lustre coating, so be sure to sprinkle *hard* enamel on the *back*, and *soft* enamel on the front. After the dish is fired and cool, examine it carefully. If the base coating has little holes or imperfections in it, sprinkle and fire it again.

Liquid metallic lustre comes in ready-to-use form in a small bottle. All you need to do is shake it throughly before using. When the dish is cool, moisten a piece of paper towelling with the carbon tetrachloride (lighter fluid) and rub it over the surface where the lustre is to be applied (in this case, the whole top surface of the dish).

Now, using a camel's-hair brush, paint a coat of gold metallic lustre over the top of the dish. When it is completely covered with an even, thin coating (when it is thick enough it will appear dark and opaque), place the dish on top of your kiln (which should be warm) to dry for several hours, preferably overnight. When the gold lustre is *thoroughly dry*, fire the dish at 1150° to 1200°F. for 2 or 3 minutes. It is almost impossible to give an exact firing time for lustres, since this varies according to the firing qualities of the base coat, but when the lustre seems bright and adheres to the surface, it is done. It is better to under-fire lustre than to risk over-firing it, so be very careful and watch the dish closely while it is in the kiln.

As we mentioned before, the previously fired counter-enamel coating will crack when you fire it again, especially when the second firing is at an extremely low temperature. This is not a problem at normal firing temperatures, but since hard-firing enamel usually requires anywhere from 1450° to 1500°F. of heat to melt, the cracks may not heal at 1200°F. If cracks form which do not heal during the first 2 minutes of the lustre firing, you will have to raise the temperature of the kiln to melt the counter-enamel so it will heal the cracks. Gold lustre will burn away at high temperatures, so raise the temperature as little as possible, and fire the dish *only until the cracks heal*. After the dish is completely fired, cool it slowly.

Sprinkle a coating of transparent red enamel on the cooled dish. Be sure that the transparent enamel coating completely covers the surface of the dish. Do not worry if the lustre starts to "crackle" while you are applying the transparent enamel coating. Now fire the dish again at 1450°F. for 2 to 4 minutes, as usual. The surface will become "crackled" during the firing process. When the transparent coating is smooth and shiny, remove and cool the dish.

The crackled surface of the dish will be very rich-looking, with a golden-red glow. You can use this technique on small areas (around edges, for example) of other enamelled objects and in combination with other techniques (such as the stencil technique), but remember to apply the lustre as the last stage of the project, and to cover the lustre with clear or colored transparent enamel during the last firing. Transparent aqua and blue enamels look best over platinum metallic lustre, and beige transparent enamel looks best over palladium metallic lustre, while red, as you have seen here, looks best over gold metallic lustre. Do not over-use metallic lustres, however, for large areas covered in metallic lustres tend to look tasteless, and a series of metallic-covered objects shows the same tasteless effect. A single, small metallic-covered object or a metallic edge is extremely effective.

This flower-shaped necklace was decorated with red and bright green enamels. The brooch was covered with enamel "splinters" (long lumps) and fired at a low (1350° F.) temperature to preserve the shape of the splinters.

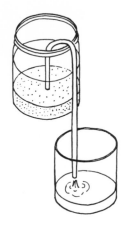
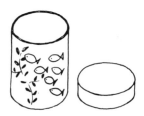

WASHING ENAMEL POWDERS

If transparent colors appear cloudy or muddy after your first firing attempts, you will have to wash them. The cloudiness is a result of impurities which have invaded the enamel powder.

Place the transparent enamel powder in a clean glass jar, such as a preserve or marmalade jar, and fill the jar with ordinary tap water. After the enamel has settled on the bottom of the jar, siphon off the water (see illustration) with a rubber tube into another jar, or carefully pour the water from one jar to another until all the impurities have been eliminated and the water is clear.

Empty the enamel on to a piece of blotting paper, and let the powder dry.

Tedious, isn't it? You can save yourself this chore by keeping your enamel powders tightly capped at all times, so that dust and other impurities cannot invade your supply.

A Silver Leaf Dish

Materials Checklist

> pre-formed copper dish, about 5 inches in diameter
> 80-mesh hard-firing dark green opaque enamel powder
> 80-mesh hard-firing pale green transparent enamel powder
> 2 to 3 sheets of silver foil
> camel's-hair brush
> sheet of tracing paper
> manicure scissors
> tracing wheel or cork stuck with several sewing needles
> facial tissue
> kitchen knife or burnisher

Adhesive Solution (as before)

Cleaning Materials (as before)

Firing Materials (as before)

Shapes made of silver or gold metallic foil (readily available from your enamelling supplier) embedded in a colored or clear transparent enamel coating are very attractive, and offer a wide variety of design possibilities. The foil shapes appear to float in a transparent sea of color over a dark background, and are among the most interesting and effective decorative accents in enamelling. The technique is basically simple, and though it requires painstaking care, it is well worth the effort.

As we have stressed before, cleanliness is one of the most essential factors in enamelling. If the metal shapes you use are not properly cleansed of all impurities, enamel will not adhere to their surfaces, and if the enamels you use are "dirty," they will look clouded and muddy after firing. When metallic foil or lustre are to be part of a design, it is essential that the transparent enamels you apply over them be utterly clean, or the metallic brilliance will not shine through the enamel, and all your work will have been wasted.

So before you begin this project, check the transparent color you plan to use and make sure it contains no specks of dirt or other impurities. If you are not sure it is perfectly clean, wash the enamel.

Before you begin, clean and polish the copper dish. When it is ready to enamel, sprinkle the back of the dish with a hard-firing dark green opaque enamel, and the front of the dish in a medium- or hard-firing dark green opaque enamel. (Remember, you may have to sprinkle and fire the dish 2 or 3 times before the base coating is complete.) During the last firing, allow the enamel almost to reach the glossy stage, as the next few firings will be at a low temperature.

While the dish is cooling, begin to prepare the silver metallic foil leaves which will form the design. (A color photograph of this dish is on page 55.) The silver metallic foil you purchase will come in sheets about 4 inches by 4 inches. The foil is so thin and fragile that it cannot be picked up with the fingers or it will disintegrate, so it must be handled and cut between 2 sheets of transparent paper, such as tracing paper. Fold a piece of tracing paper about 10 inches square in half, so you have an "envelope" a little larger than the dimensions of your sheet of foil. Before you place the foil inside the "envelope," however, draw the leaf design on the top fold of the tracing paper. This will serve as a cutting guide later on. Dampen a camel's-hair brush in a little water, and pick up the foil with the tip of the damp brush, placing the foil in between the sheets of tracing paper.

Before you cut out the leaf, it must be pricked with several tiny holes so that during the firing process the gases in the foil can escape. If you do not prick the foil it will "rise up" or lift off the enamel surface after it is fired. There are several ways to prick these tiny holes. If you have a little tracing wheel for cutting dress patterns, run the little wheel over the surface of the foil—still sandwiched between 2 pieces of tracing paper—until the surface is well pricked. Another method is to insert fine sewing needles in a cork, points down, and prick the foil right through the tracing paper in several places.

Now, using a pair of sharp, tiny scissors (manicure scissors are ideal), cut around the outlines of the leaf design you sketched before. Cut the paper-foil-paper sandwich as though it were a single piece of paper. In other words, since there are 2 layers of tracing paper and 1 layer of foil, you will be cutting

1. Place the sheet of foil between two sheets of tracing paper, prick several tiny holes to allow any gases to escape, and cut out a leaf shape using a sharp pair of scissors or a razor blade.

2. Using a slightly moistened camel's-hair brush, transfer the cut-out leaf to the previously enamelled, fired and cool adhesive-coated dish. Press the foil leaf down on the surface of the dish with a soft facial tissue, dry the dish, and fire it at 1200° F. for 1 minute.

3. After removing the dish from the kiln, tamp the leaf down with the blunt end of a kitchen knife. If the foil does not adhere to the enamel, fire the dish again briefly. Now the dish is ready to be sprinkled with transparent enamel and fired for the last time.

out 3 leaves at the same time, though only the foil leaf will be utilized on the enamelled dish. The tracing paper is only there to stiffen the foil while it is being cut and pricked. Save the foil scraps for the next project.

Coat the cooled dish with adhesive, using a camel's-hair brush. Now remove the top piece of tracing paper from the cut-out leaf, using a pair of tweezers. Lift the leaf off the bottom sheet of tracing paper with your adhesive-coated camel's-hair brush, and place it on the adhesive-coated dish.

Using a soft facial tissue, press the foil leaf down on the surface of the dish, smoothing out any wrinkles. Do this carefully, or you will break the foil. At the same time, try to blot up as much moisture from the adhesive-coated surface as possible.

Follow the same procedure with as many leaves as you plan to apply to the dish. (We applied 16 little leaves, but our dish was quite large, so 3 or 4 leaves should be sufficient for your dish, and even 1 or 2 will be quite effective.) When all the leaves are in place, set the dish aside to dry. Do not dry it in the oven, as the foil will curl up, but instead let it dry in a warm, dry place.

When the dish is thoroughly dry, fire it at 1200° to 1350°F. for about 1 minute. Remove it from the kiln, and, while the dish is still hot, tamp the leaves down with the blunt side of a kitchen knife. (Professionals use a burnisher, and the tamping-down process is called burnishing.) This burnishing process presses out the air bubbles which have accumulated during the firing process, and also presses the foil into the soft enamel. If the foil has not adhered to the enamel, fire the dish again briefly at the same temperature, repeat the burnishing process, and cool it slowly.

When the dish is cool, lightly sprinkle on a coat of transparent green enamel, and fire it at 1450°F. for about 2 to 4 minutes, or until the enamel becomes smooth and shiny. After the dish is cool you can file the edges and polish the surface.

Gold foil, also readily available in sheet form, is handled just like silver foil. A few gold foil shapes "floating" in transparent red enamel (on a tray, for example) are very dramatic and beautiful.

Making a pendant like this one is a good way to use up left-over foil scraps. Here a dark green silk cord has been used instead of a silver chain.

A Gleaming Pendant Made with "Left-Overs"

Materials Checklist

pre-formed copper pendant with hole near one edge
scraps of silver foil left over from silver leaf dish
80-mesh dark blue opaque hard-firing enamel
toothpick
camel's-hair brush
tracing paper
manicure scissors
facial tissue
80-mesh transparent pale blue enamel

Adhesive Solution (as before)

Cleaning Materials (as before)

Firing Materials (as before)

Silver foil is not inexpensive, and it would be a shame to waste the scraps left over from projects like the silver leaf dish. Fortunately, designing with bits of metallic foil is one of the most popular techniques for jewelry, so this is a wonderful way to use up your left-over scraps!

Working with scraps of foil is essentially the same as working with larger pieces. Scraps can be used to cover a piece of jewelry completely, or can be incorporated as accents into a combination of techniques for a complicated design.

Just remember to be especially careful about cleanliness when using foil. Clean and polish the copper pendant and enamel it on both sides in a dark blue hard-firing opaque enamel. Before you fire the pendant, push a toothpick or the end of a little camel's-hair brush through the hole where the jump ring will go, to clear it. (If you neglect this step the enamel coating will fuse over the hole and you will not be able to attach the jump ring.)

Fire the pendant at 1500°F. for 1 to 3 minutes, or until it reaches the wavy stage. Remove it from the kiln and allow it to cool completely.

While the pendant is cooling, prepare the foil scraps. "Sandwich" the scraps left over from the silver foil leaf dish between 2 sheets of tracing paper. Leave an inch or so around the edges of the tracing paper free of scraps so that you will have an edge to hold on to while you are cutting the scraps.

Using a pair of manicure scissors, make a series of parallel cuts through the tracing paper and its filling of little scraps. Space the cuts about $1/8$ to $1/16$ inch apart. When you have made several parallel cuts, turn the paper around and make several additional cuts at another angle. After you begin to make cuts at an angle the little scraps of foil will begin to fall out, so be sure that there is an immaculate piece of white paper underneath the immediate area to receive them. Separate the tiny scraps which have fallen out from time to time with a soft camel's-hair brush.

Now coat the cooled pendant with a rather thick adhesive solution, and, using a camel's-hair brush dipped in adhesive solution, pick up the scraps of foil one by one and begin to place then on the pendant. Space them rather close together, as the entire surface is to be covered in this case. When the pendant is covered with the scraps, press the surface lightly with a facial tissue to further affix the scraps and remove as much moisture as possible. Then set the pendant aside to dry.

1. Place the scraps of foil between two sheets of tracing paper.

2. Make a series of parallel cuts through the tracing paper with its filling of foil scraps. Then turn the tracing paper around and make another series of parallel cuts. Be sure there is a piece of immaculate white paper underneath the tracing paper to receive the foil scraps.

3. Transfer the cut-out scraps to the adhesive-coated pendant with a slightly moistened camel's-hair brush. When all the scraps are in place the pendant is ready to be dried, fired, burnished and sprinkled with transparent enamel before the final firing.

When it is completely dry, fire it at 1350° to 1400°F. for about 2 minutes. Remove it from the kiln and burnish the surface with a kitchen knife as you did when you made the silver leaf dish. If the scraps of foil fly off the surface you will have to tamp them down with a little adhesive solution, dry the pendant again, and re-fire it for a minute or so at the same temperature.

When the foil adheres tightly to the enamelled surface, cool it completely. When the pendant is cool, sprinkle on a thin coating of transparent light blue enamel. (A thick layer of enamel would look cloudy and obscure the brilliance of the foil after firing.) Fire the pendant at 1450° to 1500°F. for 2 minutes or so. If after it is fired and cool you feel it needs a little more color, sprinkle on another extremely thin layer of transparent blue enamel and re-fire it. Two thin coats are always better than one thick coat.

When the pendant is finished, file the edges and polish it. Attach a jump ring and a chain from your selection of findings and it is ready to wear.

As you will see, foil "left-overs" can be made into lovely pieces of jewelry, so save all your scraps. Foil scraps can also be incorporated into other techniques—in backgrounds or as accents. Just use your imagination as you go along, and add foil scraps whenever they would enhance an especially beautiful piece.

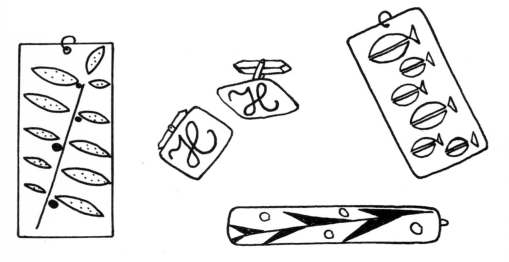

Glass jewels may even be fused only partially to an enamel surface, so that they appear to be floating off the object. Be sure that at least half the jewel is fused to the enamel, however, or it may pop off later on.

A Jewelled Brooch

Materials Checklist

1 large glass marble
pre-formed copper brooch
steel firing stilt
flat steel plate for firing support
pail of cold water
80-mesh light colored medium-firing opaque enamel powder
glass container with lid
camel's-hair brush

Adhesive Solution (as before)
Cleaning Materials (as before)
Firing Materials (as before)

How would you like to manufacture your own "jewels" from such unlikely things as old beer and wine bottles or marbles? Several years ago an American enamellist devised a way to do this easily. With very little effort you can produce wonderfully shaped and colored "jewels" and add them to your enamelled creations for even more individuality and scope.

Such diverse things as broken tail-lights from your car and medicine bottles

83

can be used to make jewels. Collecting as many odd pieces of glass as you can find will probably become almost another hobby. The simplest thing to begin with is an ordinary child's glass marble, and this is how to make a single marble into a hundred jewels:

Pre-heat your kiln to 1700° to 1800°F. Place the marble on a steel firing stand (bottles and larger scraps of glass may be placed on an old metal screen instead). Fire the marble (watching it closely) and withdraw it as soon as it is red-hot and showing signs of melting and changing its shape. Fill a pail with cold water and, using your enamelling fork and wearing gloves, plunge the red-hot marble—still on its firing stand—into the cold water. (When working with larger chunks of glass on a screen, plunge them into the water without trying to remove them from the screen, as they sometimes stick until they are cool.) Guard yourself, especially your eyes.

After the marble has been heated until it is red hot, it is removed from the kiln with tongs and plunged into a bucket of cold water, where it will shatter into hundreds of tiny pieces.

As the red-hot marble comes into contact with the cold water it will shatter into hundreds of little pieces, making a very loud noise. This is the process which will turn the tiny pieces of glass into smooth round jewels when they are re-fired. (If you simply hammered the marble into tiny pieces and then fired the pieces they would just melt and remain shapeless no matter how many times you fired them.)

Empty the water from the pail, and turn out the glass fragments on a piece of paper towelling. (Clean the pail with a thick towel—not your bare fingers! —to remove any stray pieces of glass before re-using.) When the pieces are completely dry, store them in a glass container, to be made into little jewels as you need them.

These tiny fragments of glass will be transformed into miniature jewels after a second firing.

To make the jewelled brooch, shake 8 or 10 little glass pieces out of the jar, and, using tweezers, place them on a flat steel firing support, spacing them ¼ inch or so apart (so they will not fuse together). Fire them at 1700°F. until they become round and smooth. Watching this process is very exciting—it seems almost a miracle that rough slivers of glass will form themselves into such pretty and varied little shapes.

When the jewels are formed, remove them from the kiln on the firing stand, and, using a spatula, slide them off the firing stand on to an asbestos brick where they will cool.

The finished jewels.

Now prepare the brooch to receive the jewels. Lay the jewels experimentally on the brooch. If you have more jewels than you will need for the brooch, store the extras in a glass jar and cover them with water until you use them. Set the jewels aside, and clean, polish and enamel the brooch on both sides in a single, hard-firing opaque enamel powder. When the brooch is fired and cool, place the jewels back on the face of the brooch in an interesting design or as

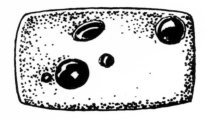

The finished brooch. Glass jewels can be made to seem even more luminous by placing a tiny scrap of silver foil under each jewel before firing.

accents, holding them in place with a little adhesive solution applied with a brush. Dry the brooch, and fire it at 1450° to 1500°F. briefly. Watch it carefully while it is in the kiln, and remove it as soon as the jewels are fused to the enamel surface, for if you leave the brooch in the kiln too long the jewels will melt into the enamel coating.

When the brooch is cool, file and polish the edges, and cement a catch from your selection of findings on the back.

Glass jewels have almost unlimited uses in enamelling. You can use them as single accents as you have done here, or pile several all together in the middle of an ash tray, for example, and fuse them together. As time goes on and your glass collection grows, you will think of hundreds of ways in which to use them.

Delicate gold stars in cloisonné look particularly striking on this dark green candleholder.

The finished ash tray can be coated with clear nail polish to protect the colors and prevent further oxidation, but enamel is so durable that this step is not essential.

A Simple Cloisonné Ash Tray

Materials Checklist

pre-formed copper ash tray, square, flat shape
80-mesh opaque enamel powder, hard-firing
fine silver cloisonné wire
pair of round-nosed pliers
pair of tweezers
distilled water
sharp knife, toothpick or pointer, small spatula or spreader

Adhesive Solution (as before)

Cleaning Materials (acid or vinegar solution) (as before)

Firing Materials (as before)

The cloisonné technique consists of separating areas of applied enamel colors with very fine wire, each color forming its own partition, or cell

These delightful cloisonné ash trays are examples of the simple designs it is best to work with until you are skilled in the technique.

Simple cloisonné designs are often more effective than complicated, fussy— and extremely difficult— designs, so do not feel limited by them.

The best way to obtain an even enamel coating is to tap the slightly inclined shaker with your index finger instead of shaking your whole hand. (You can improvise enamel shakers by cementing a piece of 80-mesh screening inside plastic medicine tubes.)

(cloison). As you have noticed, enamel colors tend to run together, in that, with most techniques, there is no sharply defined division of colors after firing. The cloisonné technique, however, permits precise and dramatic color contrasts by separating different colors with wire barriers.

After assembling the necessary materials, clean the copper ash tray with acid or with vinegar-salt-water solution. The ash tray will look better if you

This bracelet is a multi-colored cloisonné design in pale violet, pink and green.

clean it with acid solution, but if you are working with children you can use the vinegar solution with only a slight loss in brilliance. When the ash tray is perfectly clean, enamel it on both sides in a single color of hard opaque enamel. (We used dark blue.) Remember to under-fire it, since it will be fired at least 6 times—2 or 3 now, and 3 or 4 times when you apply the design. While it is cooling, prepare the cloisonné design in the following manner:

MAKING A CLOISONNÉ DESIGN

For this first cloisonné project we have chosen the simplest of motifs, a white sailboat on a blue background. Complicated designs in cloisonné require great skill, so it is important to avoid them until you are expert in this technique. Intersections and crossings of wire and long straight lines are not advisable, since they tend to incline and lose their shape when fired, so the best designs to use at first are flat decorative forms, such as fishes, flowers, birds and boats.

When you buy cloisonné wire (be sure to buy fine silver cloisonné wire as it does not turn black during firing), "anneal" it when you receive it by placing the whole length of wire in your kiln or an open flame until the wire turns red. This process will help the wire hold its shape while you are cutting, applying and firing it.

When you have decided upon your design, trace its outline on a piece of white paper. With a pair of round-nosed pliers, cut pieces of cloisonné wire to fit the sketched design, and lay them over the design as you go along.

APPLYING A CLOISONNÉ DESIGN

Dip the pieces of wire, holding them with a pair of tweezers, into a thick adhesive solution, and carefully place them in position on the ash tray one at a time. When they are all in place on the ash tray, slide your enamelling fork or spatula gently under the ash tray, and fire it for 1 or 2 minutes at 1550°F. The wires will sink down into the base coat, and will be fixed permanently to the metal. When the ash tray is cool you will be able to fill the cells (cloisons) which you have created with the wire design.

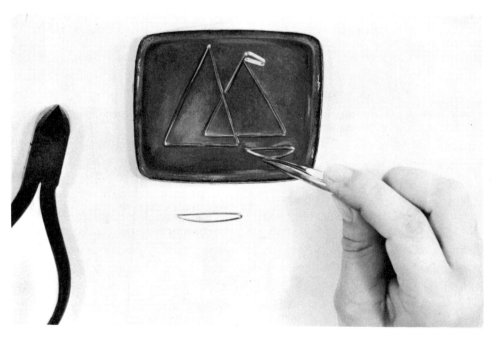

Glue the cut-out and annealed wire sections to the previously enamelled and fired ash tray, one by one.

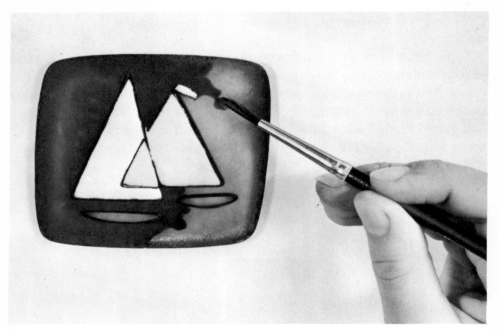

After the enamel powders are mixed with adhesive solution, they are applied with a brush, spreader or even a toothpick around and inside the wire "cells."

WET APPLICATION OF ENAMEL

Since you want to apply enamel to restricted areas, you cannot sprinkle it as you have done when enamelling an object completely, so you will use what is known as the "wet application" technique to "control" the enamel application. To do this, mix a small amount of enamel powder in the colors you have chosen for the cloisonné design (dark blue background and a white sailboat in this case) with a few drops of adhesive solution or distilled water (tap water contains impurities and will fade the colors), until the enamel is moist enough to spread easily. The enamel will resemble a moist pap when it is the right consistency.

With a tiny spatula (or professional "spreader"), pick up a small amount of white enamel pap and spread it inside one of the cells in the design. Fill the large outside areas of your design with blue enamel pap right up to the top of the wires. Then, using a toothpick or a "pointer," fill the small areas and tiny corners of your design with the wet enamel pap. Do not be afraid to use a brush, or even a little stick for large areas. Use the "tools" you feel most comfortable with, as long as you have rinsed them in the cleaning solution so that they are "clean" and free of oil.

When you have filled the cells up to the top with wet enamel, the ash tray is ready to dry. If you fire it before the wet enamel is dry, the water with which

After the ash tray is thoroughly dried, it is placed in the kiln and fired at 1500° F. for three minutes. If the enamel sinks down below the surface of the wires, more enamel pap is applied, the ash tray is re-dried and then re-fired.

After the ash tray is fired and cool, the surface is polished. If a bright, glossy sheen is desired use a "glass brush" like this one instead of a carborundum rubbing stone to polish the wires and to remove any traces of excess enamel around the edges of the cells.

you mixed the powdered enamel will boil during the high-temperature firing process, causing the enamel to spill over the wire barriers. So, put the ash tray in a very low-temperature kitchen oven until all the water has evaporated. This should take 25 to 45 minutes. Then fire the ash tray in your kiln at 1500°F. for about 3 minutes. You will probably find that the enamel in the cells has shrunk below the surface of the wires in the firing process, so fill the cells with wet enamel pap once again, following the same procedure. Dry the ash tray and fire it again. To avoid still a third application, be sure to fill the cells as high as possible the second time. You can file away any excess enamel after the ash tray is fired and cool. At this time you should also polish the surface and the wires under water with your carborundum rubbing stone.

Transparent green ivy leaves in cloisonné nestle on the red enamel background of this box.

This perfectly simple ash tray is your first step towards the exotic and complicated Chinese cloisonné works of art which are preserved in museums throughout the world. With a little experience and imagination you can develop cloisonné designs which are intricate and fascinating.

Abstract cloisonné motifs are especially suited to small areas, such as the links of this handsome bracelet.

(Above) This necklace was made by enamelling five copper squares in different sizes in an abstract cloisonné motif. Each square had two holes, through which jump rings were attached. The squares were linked together by the jump rings, and fastened to a silver chain. (Left) These cheerful cuff links are bright red cloisonné cherries on a white background.

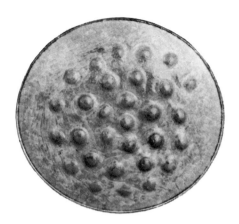

This sky blue dish has a pock-marked, lunar surface. After it was removed from the kiln in a red-hot state, the round depressions were embossed into the soft enamel with a blunt-edged chasing tool.

(Left and below) These copper plaques are fine examples of the special effects obtained when enamel is "pulled" with a scrolling iron during the firing process. Bunsen burners are indicated for this technique, because the plaques must be exposed during firing to obtain this effect.

(Above) The champlevé technique is another way to separate colors. Instead of creating wire barriers, as in cloisonné, depressions are etched out of a metal surface and then filled with enamel. The end result is not as precise as cloisonné separation. This technique is best attempted by expert enamellists. Here a design is painted on a square of copper with black asphalt paint. The paint will protect those surfaces which are not to be etched out, so the back and sides of the copper square are also covered with black asphalt paint.

THE CHAMPLEVÉ TECHNIQUE

(Right) After the asphalt paint is thoroughly dry, the square is immersed in a glass container which is first half-filled with water and then filled with nitric acid. The square must be left in the acid bath for about ten hours, or until about $\frac{1}{16}$ of an inch of metal has been eaten away. The occasional air bubbles which form during the etching process must be brushed away with a feather. When the square is etched, it is removed and thoroughly rinsed in cold running water.

Now the etched parts of the metal, called champlevé excavations, are filled with wet enamel just as in the cloisonné technique. After the enamel is dry, the square is fired at 1500° F. for 2 to 4 minutes, and, if necessary, the process is repeated until the excavations are completely filled. A series of copper squares like this could be cemented to pieces of wood and set into table tops or trays.

(Right) This bracelet was enamelled in two steps: first it was covered completely with wet enamel (dry enamel would not cling to the steep sides), dried and fired. Next, transparent enamel flowers were "painted" on, using the Limoges technique. The bracelet was dried and fired again.

Common Flaws After Firing
and How to Correct Them

CRACKS AND FISSURES:

CAUSE: Too thick a layer of enamel or uneven application of enamel, especially with transparent enamels and when enamelling on extremely thin copper. The difference in the expansion and contraction rates during the firing and cooling processes causes great tension, and can lead to such cracks.

RESTORATION: Refiring, and possibly the application of counter-enamel.

ENAMEL FLIES OFF THE OBJECT IN LARGE CHIPS

CAUSE: Perhaps the sheet-copper was too thin, or the enamel layer too thick. Perhaps the wong kind of enamel was used or the object was not properly "cleaned" before enamelling.

RESTORATION: Dust chipped places with enamel after a thorough cleaning process and refire. Thin copper must be counter-enamelled.

BUBBLES AND PIN-PRICK PORES ON ENAMEL LAYER

CAUSE: Water in the wet enamel application was not given a chance to evaporate completely prior to firing; the metal was not cleaned properly, or the firing temperature was too high.

RESTORATION: Carefully file bubbles away; dust porous enamel layer again and refire.

BURNT HOLES

CAUSE: Enamel layer was too thin, firing temperature too high.

RESTORATION: In cases of opaque enamel, dust and fire again. Transparent enamel will have burned away, so sprinkle on a completely new layer after filing away the holes and any oxidation.

BLACK EDGES
CAUSE: Firing was too intense and too long.

RESTORATION: None. Try filing the black edges away, but you will probably be unsuccessful in salvaging the piece.

ROUGH AND UNEVEN ENAMEL
CAUSE: Firing time was too short and at too low a temperature.

RESTORATION: Fire the object once again at a higher temperature.

DISCOLORATION
CAUSE: White enamel sometimes shows green spots and edges, and red enamel occasionally displays black stains. These are oxidation stains, which result from an exceedingly high temperature or an overlong firing.

RESTORATION: Sprinkle the object again and fire it at a lower temperature.

OPAQUE ENAMELS TURN TRANSPARENT
CAUSE: The firing was too intense.

RESTORATION: None.

WARPING
CAUSE: Several firings and/or intense heat.

RESTORATION: Place heavy steel object on top of a flat object during cooling. Wearing asbestos gloves, after the hot metal cools for a minute or so, turn a bowl or curved dish upside down and press its rim against a flat concrete or metal surface to restore shape.

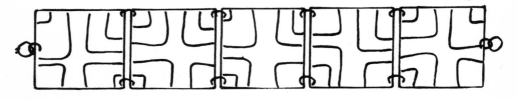

Index

Acid cleaning solution,
  60–63
  how to store, 64
Adhesive, "painting" with,
  45–46
  preparation of, 18–19
Application of powdered
  enamel, 8–9
Applying design techniques,
  47, 58
Ash tray, textured, 37–41
Base coat, application of,
  27–28
Bowl, counter-enamelled,
  32–36
Bracelet, sgraffito, 65–66
Brooch, jewelled, 83–86
Bunsen and butane gas
  burners, 16–17
Carborundum rubbing
  stone, 31–94
Cellini, Benvenuto, 5, 6
Champlevé technique in
  pictures, 98–100
Cleaning materials, 7
Cleaning metal, 8
  with vinegar, 8
  with dry acid, 60–61
  with nitric acid, 60–63
Cloisonné technique, 87–95
  applying the design, 91
  making the design, 90
  wet application of
    enamel, 92–93

Coasters, stencilled, 27–30
Color photographs, 48–56
Common Flaws After Firing
  and How to Correct
  them, 101–102
Cooling fired enamel, 10–11
Correcting firing flaws,
  101–102
Counter-enamel, commer-
  cial, 44
Counter-enamelling, 32–36
  one side at a time, 36
  simultaneous, 33–36
Crackle technique, 70–73
Cuff links, abstract, 60–64
Design techniques
  champlevé, 98–100
  cloisonné, 87–95
  crackle (metallic lustres),
    70–73
  dry brushing, 67
  glass jewels, 83–86
  how to choose, 47, 58
  Limoges, 71
  lumps and threads,
    37–44
  masking, 60–64
  metallic foil, 75–82
  sgrafitto, 65–66
  stencil, 27–30
  with firing characteris-
    tics, 57–58
Dish, nut, 57–58
Dish, silver leaf, 75–78

Drying enamel, 35
Earrings, geometric, 67–69
Enamel (s), 5
  ancient examples of, 4, 6,
    48, 52
  application of, 8–9
  cooling after firing,
    10–11
  drying before firing, 35
  firing characteristics, 24
  hard-firing, 24, 38,
    57–58, 72
  kinds of, 21
  labelling, 22
  lumps and threads,
    37–44
  medium-firing, 24, 38
  mixing, 23
  opalescent, 21
  opaque, 21
  purchase of, 21
  samples, making, 25
  soft-firing, 24, 38,
    57–58, 72
  storing, 22–23
  threads, pulled, 42
  transparent, 21
  under-firing, 35
  washing, 74
Enamelling on an acid-
  cleaned surface, 63
Filing, 31
Findings, 12
Fire scale, 31

103

Firing enamel, 9–10, 24
  cooling after, 10–11
  cracking during, 46–47
  drying before, 35
  flaws, correcting,
    101–102
  materials, 7
  stilts, 10, 17, 34, 35
  tools, 19
  under-firing, 35
  wavy stage, 35
Flowered Pen-and-Pencil
  Tray, 43
Foil, metallic, 75–82
  applying, 76–78
  burnishing, 78
  cutting, 76–77
  firing, 78
  scraps, how to use, 79–81
Gay Counter-Enamelled
  Bowl, 32–36
Glass-domed kilns, 15–16
Glass jewels, 83–86
Gleaming Pendant made
  with Left-Overs, 79–82
Golden Crackle Plate, 70–73
Gold foil—see Foil
Hard-firing enamels, 24, 38,
  57–58, 72
Introduction, 5
Jewelled Brooch, 83–86
Jewels, glass, 83–86
Kilns, 15–18
  Bunsen and butane gas
    burners, 16–17
  glass-domed, 15–16

  larger, 17
Limoges technique, 71
Liquid metallic lustres,
  70–73
Luminous Leaf Brooch, 45
Lumps and threads, 37–44
Making a Simple Pendant, 7
Masking technique, 60–64
Matchbox, 42
Medium-firing enamel,
  24, 38
Metallic foil—see Foil
Metallic lustres, 70–73
Metal parts, pre-formed,
  12–13
Metal, pickling or
  cleaning, 8
  with vinegar, 8
  with dry acid, 60–61
  with nitric acid, 60–63
Nut dish, veined, 57–58
Opalescent enamel, 21
Opaque enamel, 21, 24
Other equipment, 20
"Painting" with adhesive,
  45–46
Pair of Geometric Earrings,
  67–69
Pendant, simple, 7
Pickling metal, 8
  with vinegar, 8
  with dry acid, 60–61
  with nitric acid, 60–63
Plate, golden crackle, 70–73
Pre-formed parts, 12–13
"Professional" Abstract

  Cuff Links, 60–64
"Scratched" Link Bracelet,
  65–66
Sgraffito technique, 65–66
Silver foil—see Foil
Silver Leaf Dish, 75
Soft-firing enamel, 24, 38,
  57–58, 72
Soldering, 68–69
Stencil design, application
  of, 28–29
Stencilled Coasters, 27–30
Stencils, how to make, 28
Stilts, firing, 10, 17, 34, 35
"Surprise" Textured Ash
  Tray, 37–41
Techniques—see Design
  Techniques
Threads, and lumps, 37–44
Three-dimensional effect,
  43–44
Tools, firing, 19
Transparent enamel, 21, 24
Tray, pen-and-pencil, 43–44
Under-firing enamel, 35
Vinegar cleaning solution, 8
Washing enamel powders,
  74
Wavy stage, 35
Wet application of enamel,
  92–93
What Is Enamel? 5
What You Will Need,
  12–20